Praelections delivered before the Senate
of the University of Cambridge,
25, 26, 27 January 1906

T0345377

Praelections delivered before the Senate
of the University of Cambridge,
25, 26, 27 January 1906

CAMBRIDGE :
at the University Press
1906

CAMBRIDGE UNIVERSITY PRESS
Cambridge, New York, Melbourne, Madrid, Cape Town,
Singapore, São Paulo, Delhi, Tokyo, Mexico City

Cambridge University Press
The Edinburgh Building, Cambridge CB2 8RU, UK

Published in the United States of America by Cambridge University Press, New York

www.cambridge.org
Information on this title: www.cambridge.org/9781107648111

First published 1906
First paperback edition 2011

A catalogue record for this publication is available from the British Library

ISBN 978-1-107-64811-1 Paperback

STATUTE FOR THE REGIUS PROFESSORSHIPS OF DIVINITY, HEBREW AND GREEK.

Approved by the Queen in Council, 10 *May,* 1860.

Every candidate shall, on a day to be assigned by the Electors, expound openly in the Public Schools for the space of one hour, a part of Holy Scripture, or of a book written in the Hebrew or Greek language, according as the Professorship vacant is that of Divinity, Hebrew, or Greek; such part of Holy Scripture, or of a book written in the Hebrew or Greek language, being assigned to him by the Electors.

TRINITY HALL LODGE, 22 *January*, 1906.

THE VICE-CHANCELLOR begs leave to inform Members of the Senate that the following Candidates for the Regius Professorship of Greek will, at the times undermentioned, respectively expound openly in the Senate House the following parts of books written in the Greek language :

Dr ADAM,—Thursday, January 25, 5 P.M.

καὶ σῶμα μὲν πάντων ἕπεται θανάτῳ περισθενεῖ,
ζωὸν δ' ἔτι λείπεται αἰῶνος εἴδωλον· τὸ γάρ ἐστι μόνον
ἐκ θεῶν· εὕδει δὲ πρασσόντων μελέων, ἀτὰρ εὑδόντεσσιν
            ἐν πολλοῖς ὀνείροις
δείκνυσι τερπνῶν ἐφέρποισαν χαλεπῶν τε κρίσιν.
                    PINDAR, *fragment* 131 Bergk.

Dr WALTER HEADLAM,—Friday, January 26, 5 P.M.

AESCHYLUS, *Agamemnon*, the second Chorus, beginning line 367 (Wecklein).

Dr JACKSON,—Thursday, January 25, 2.30 P.M.

PLATO, *Cratylus*, and, in particular, chapters 42—44, 435 D—440 E.

Professor RIDGEWAY,—Saturday, January 27, 11 A.M.

AESCHYLUS, *Supplices*, 304 sqq. (Tucker) [327 sqq. (Paley)]:
    τί φῂς ἱκνεῖσθαι τῶνδ' ἀγωνίων θεῶν κτλ.

Dr VERRALL,—Friday, January 26, 2.30 P.M.

AESCHYLUS, *Eumenides*, 734—743 (Dindorf) [737—746 (Wecklein)]:
    ἐμὸν τόδ' ἔργον......τέλος (*The Vote of Athena*).

CONTENTS

HENRY JACKSON

PLATO'S CRATYLUS

PLATO'S CRATYLUS.

Mr Vice-Chancellor and Members of the Senate,

In accordance with statute, and by assignment of the electors, I am to-day to expound Plato's *Cratylus*, and, in particular the three concluding chapters. In so doing, I shall endeavour, primarily, to show that this dialogue, which on the face of it deals with a fundamental problem of philology and is commonly regarded from a purely philological standpoint, makes important contributions to the history of philosophy, and marks an epoch in Plato's philosophical development. But here, as elsewhere, the threads of Plato's discourse are as closely interwoven as the plot and the by-plot of a well-constructed play or story : and I shall not be able altogether to ignore the philological discussion. Nor am I sorry that this is so : for, though I am no philologist, I seem to myself, here too, to have something to say.

Three persons take part in the conversation : Socrates, Hermogenes, and Cratylus. Socrates is protagonist : not the Socrates of history, the moralist and the dialectician who despaired of philosophy and science; but an idealized Socrates, a Socrates possessed by an intense intellectual curiosity and endowed with a remarkable aptitude for metaphysic,—in a word, Plato himself. Of the two respondents, the one, Hermogenes, is an unimportant member of the Socratic circle, a man of good family, who, as Cratylus unkindly reminds him, despite his name, which signifies 'the child of luck,' has tried to make money and has failed to do so. His efforts in argument are, perhaps, not much more successful than his speculations in the agora. The other, Cratylus, is the belated representative of a bygone philosophy. Towards the end of the five hundreds,—say forty years before the birth of Socrates, eighty years before the birth of Plato, a hundred and twenty years before this dialogue was written,— Heracleitus of Ephesus had affirmed that all things are in perpetual flux; that nothing is stable; that so-called 'being' is but 'becoming.' Furthermore, he had recognized that that which is in perpetual flux cannot be known, and he had thus given a new direction to Greek thought. For, whereas hitherto men had fearlessly asked themselves 'What is Being?', they now saw that another question—'What is Knowledge?' was equally important, and more pressing. Heracleitus' theory of flux, having played its part in the making of thought, passed away about 500, and was succeeded by Parmenides' theory of rest. From this came, on the one hand, the logic of Zeno of Elea, and on the other, the science of Empedocles, Anaxagoras, and the Atomists. Then, about the middle of the four hundreds, the old learning, both the philosophy and the science, gave way before the humanism of the sophists. And now, towards the end of the four hundreds, Heracleiteanism reappears: but about its revival historians tell us little more than that the new Heracleiteans were more Heracleitean than Heracleitus himself, and that Plato, in his callow youth, had from Cratylus his first lessons in philosophy. It is this Cratylus with whom the Platonizing Socrates here measures his strength.

And now I will very briefly trace the argument of the dialogue. Primarily and ostensibly, it deals with the question—'Wherein does the rightness of names consist?' Cratylus and Hermogenes entertain rival theories, and Socrates moderates between them. According to Cratylus, each thing has a name naturally appropriated to it; that is to say, a name which carries in its etymology a description of the thing named, and thus of right belongs to it, and to it alone : the natural rightness of the name is the same for Greeks and Barbarians alike : appellations which depend on convention only are not names. According to Hermogenes, the thing has its name, not by nature, but by law or custom : its rightness is a mere matter of convention : names may be changed at pleasure by the community and by the individual. The rival theories having been stated, Socrates proceeds to cross-examine, and Hermogenes is his first respondent. The outcome of their conversation is, not so much a criticism of Hermogenes' contention, as rather a provisional statement of the position which Socrates takes up against Cratylus, his real opponent : and that position may be formulated as follows. Just as a proposition purports to describe a fact, but may represent it either truly or falsely, so a name purports to declare and distinguish the reality or nature of a thing, but the description which the name affords may be either true or false. In this sense things have names naturally appropriated to them : and accordingly the name-giver is, not, as Hermogenes supposes, any casual person, but an artist or professional, who, having the natural name in view, expresses the thing in suitable letters and syllables. Nevertheless, so long as the reality of the thing is duly expressed, name-givers in framing names may make use of different sounds in Greece and in Barbaria. Having laid down these principles, Socrates proceeds to illustrate and apply them in particular instances, and, for each of a considerable number of words, propounds an etymology— or, it may be, etymologies—declaratory of the nature of the thing named. In the course of these particular investigations it appears that some names are more right than others; that different combinations of letters may be used to describe the same nature ; that for the sake of euphony, by way of ornament, and through the lapse of time, letters may be added, substituted, or dropped, and accents and breathings may be altered ; that the hopes and the opinions of the name-giver may affect his nomenclature,—for example, very many names seem to presume the theory of flux; and, finally, that in these ways many names, originally significant of the natures of the things, have been so completely transformed that they are now absolutely unintelligible, or even suggest wholly different natures. Indeed it would almost seem that any name may be fitted to any thing. In default of etymological explanation, some words may perhaps be regarded as loans from barbarous languages : but plainly this is no explanation, just as it is no explanation to say that a name has a divine origin, or that its origin is lost in the mists of antiquity.

Thus far, certain primary names, such as ἰόν, ῥέον, δέον, ἔχον,—'going,' 'flowing,' 'binding,' 'staying,'— have been taken for granted : but, manifestly, if the theory is to hold its own, these primaries also should have a natural rightness, and must be interpreted through their component letters. How are we then to connect the elementary characteristics of primary things with the elementary letters which occur in primary names ?

If we were to be deprived of speech, we should indicate things and their actions—for example, a horse galloping—by imitating the thing and its action with our own persons. Even so, thinks Socrates, in speech, we indicate certain sorts of action by imitating them with the vocal parts of the person, that is to say, the mouth and the tongue ; and then the sounds produced by those imitative movements of the mouth and tongue are associated with, and signify, the several sorts of action. For example, the letter ῥῶ, which is produced by a quaking movement of the tongue, is found in words indicative of movement, such as τρέχειν, ῥοή, τρόμος, τραχύς, ἐρείκειν—'run,' 'rush,' 'tremble,' 'rough,' 'rend': λάμβδα, since in producing the sound the tongue slips, appears in words which imply slipping ; δέλτα and ταῦ, sounds which we make by pressing and squeezing the tongue against the teeth, occur in words which describe hindrance and stoppage ; γάμμα, a sound produced when the tongue slips and is arrested, is common in such words as γλίσχρον, γλοιῶδες, 'glutinous': and so forth, for I do not care to go through the whole of Plato's list.

In short, the sounds produced by certain movements of the vocal organs are associated with similar movements in general: out of these rudimentary sounds are built up primary names to represent things of which certain movements are characteristic: and, finally, out of the primary names, secondary, derivative, names are constructed to denote other things. But we are warned, first, that, even if the name-giver rightly apprehended and adequately expressed the characteristics of the thing, euphony, ornamentation, and time, may have obscured his meaning; and, secondly, that the name-giver may have been wrong in his characterization, or clumsy in the expression of it: so that the name as we have it does not necessarily show how the name-giver conceived the thing, and certainly must not be assumed to describe it correctly.

At this point Cratylus takes Hermogenes' place as respondent. Cratylus has already heard about these things from others, and thought about them for himself, and he is ready to give a general assent to Socrates' exposition. In particular, he holds with Socrates, that the rightness of a name consists in its declaration of the nature of the thing, and that names exist with a view to such declaration; that there is an art of naming; and that there are persons who practise that art. Further, the theory of the equivalence of letters and actions, which apparently is new to him, receives his cordial approval: and the remark that very many names signify movement, obviously flatters his Heracleitean prepossessions. There is however one element in Socrates' system which Cratylus emphatically disallows. He cannot admit that some name-givers are more skilful than others, and that, accordingly, some names are better, others worse. All names, he thinks, are good : appellations which are not good, are not names. For example, Hermocrates—'Fortunatus,' or 'Felix'—is not the name of the unlucky speculator who bears it : it is the name of some one who has prospered in life. In a word, Cratylus regards a false proposition as non-significant, and, in like manner, an inappropriate name as an empty sound. Socrates replies at length, and by a careful and cogent argument obliges Cratylus to confess that he has nothing to say for himself. But, though silenced, he is not convinced.

Socrates drops the matter, and turns to another. He gets Cratylus to admit that in the word σκληρότης, 'hardness,' the letter λάμβδα, which suggests 'softness,' is out of place, and that it is in virtue of custom or convention that he and Socrates understand one another when this word is used between them. But again, though silenced, Cratylus is not convinced. He still thinks that the name of a thing, not only purported in the first instance to describe the thing, but also, if it *is* a name, continues to do so. No, says Socrates firmly : the name indicates the thing whether the components of the name recall or do not recall the thing's characteristics : and, if this is so, we must needs acknowledge that it is not the likeness of the name to the thing which makes the name indicative of it, but custom or convention.

In the argument which I have summarized, Cratylus is routed at every turn. This being so, his persistence in the assertion of what is indefensible, can only mean that the dogma in question was seriously entertained by the real Cratylus. In other words, the theory that names, if they really are names and not mere sounds, represent the nature or reality of things, must be regarded as an article of the later Heracleiteanism. Hereupon the attentive reader asks himself—'How is it that this dogma finds a place in a philosophy which did so much—perhaps more than any other—to overthrow the old philosophy and the old science, and to bring about the sceptical crisis and the humanist triumph of the middle of the four hundreds? Why is it that the representative of this revolutionary philosophy is so keenly interested in the retention of this particular philosopheme?' In the study of human intelligence, as in the study of physical development, difficulties, exceptions, anomalies, are always of supreme importance to the inquirer, not only because, in Plato's phrase, they are 'provocative of thought,' but also because they indicate that something hitherto ignored is an element in the problem. With this remark, I take up again my summary at 433 D.

Tell me next, says Socrates, what it is that names do. They convey information, says Cratylus. He who knows names, knows also, in virtue of their resemblance to things, the things which they represent; and this is true, not only of one who learns from another, but also of one who discovers for himself: the study of names is the best, and the only, way of investigating things. An insecure procedure, replies Socrates: for plainly the original name-giver framed the name in accordance with his conception of the thing, and his conception may have been erroneous. No, says Cratylus: the name-giver had knowledge: as I have already explained, appellations not based upon knowledge are not names : and that the name-giver has done his work correctly, appears in the consistency of his nomenclature : you yourself re-marked that his names are framed on the same principle and point to the same conclusion, the theory of flux. That, retorts Socrates, is no justification : it is quite conceivable that the name-giver started from a wrong principle, and then framed all his names in accordance with it : moreover, it may be doubted whether all names *are* thus consistent : hitherto we have supposed that the significance of names depends upon the principle of flux ; for example, at 412 A, we conjectured, in accordance with the theory of flux, that ἐπιστήμη was derived from ἕπομαι and ought to be pronounced with an aspirate, ἑπιστήμη ; but it is just as plausible to derive it, in accordance with the theory of rest, from ἐφίστημι : and a host of words which we have explained by the theory of flux may be quite as well explained by the theory of rest. A majority of etymologies, says Cratylus, point to the theory of flux. Socrates scoffs at this appeal to statistics, and Cratylus has nothing to say in its defence.

It is now plain why it was that Cratylus cared so much for his philological theory. It was because he claimed to obtain through names that knowledge of things which he despaired of obtaining through the senses.

According to Cratylus, continues Socrates at 438 A, the giver of the primary names, when he made them, already knew the things which were to be named. But if it is only through names that things can be known, the name-giver could not know things, so long as there were no names through which to know them. Surely it is obvious that realities must be studied in themselves, and not in names, which are at best copies of them.

Having by this time completely overborne the resistance of Cratylus, Socrates proceeds at 439 B to dispute, not indeed the theory of flux, but the theory that flux is universal. There are, he thinks, such things as a self-beautiful, and a self-good, and other like unities : and, whereas particular things which are beautiful and particular things which are good, being subject to flux, are also respectively unbeautiful and evil, the self-beautiful and the self-good are always true to their natures. Now, that which is in flux cannot be known because it is not a stable, determinate, object : and, if flux is universal, there can be no knowledge whatever, because, ex hypothesi, there is no stable, determinate, subject. On the other hand, if there is a subject which knows, and an object which is known, the beautiful, the good, and the other unities,—if they are that object,—must needs be exempt from flux. It is no easy matter, thinks Socrates, to choose between these alternatives : but it is irrational to rely upon names for a proof that flux is universal. Cratylus makes a final declaration of loyalty to Heracleitus, and so the dialogue ends.

What then is Plato's moral? In the *Cratylus*, as in other dialogues, he is at no pains to set out explicitly the lesson which he desires to inculcate. But this much is clear : he invites us to choose between two theories : the theory of the Heracleiteans that flux is universal, which theory, he thinks, makes knowledge impossible ; and his own theory, that, distinct from things which are in flux and unknowable, there are existent unities, such as the self-beautiful and the self-good, which, being stable, are capable of being known.

In other words, whereas Cratylus maintains that *all* things are in flux, and unknowable in themselves, but nevertheless knowable through their names, Plato, —holding that sensible things are in flux and therefore unknowable, but denying Cratylus' theory of knowledge,—in order that there may be objects of knowledge, postulates eternal, immutable, unities, distinct from the transient, mutable, pluralities of sense. That is to say, he enunciates what was, alike in the *republic* and in the *Timaeus*, the fundamental proposition of his theory of ideas : and he comes to this fundamental proposition in exactly the way which Aristotle describes in the *metaphysics*, M iv ; "the supporters of the theory of ideas," says Aristotle, "were brought to it by their acceptance of the Heracleitean principle that all sensibles are in perpetual flux, so that if there is to be any knowledge of any thing or any understanding, there must needs be, distinct from natures which are sensible, other natures which are stable." I can imagine no better or clearer statement of the result reached in the *Cratylus* than these sentences of Aristotle's. It is possible that he was thinking of the *Cratylus* as he wrote them.

In this dialogue then the two contemporary philosophies are brought face to face, and accordingly I shall have something to say about its bearings upon both of them. In discussing its relations to Heracleiteanism, I shall in some sort pursue an old track, inasmuch as Ferdinand Lassalle, the socialist— Mr Meredith's tragic comedian—and other scholars of repute, have recognized the importance of the *Cratylus* as an authority for that philosophy. Nevertheless, if I am not mistaken, my conclusions are new. In discussing the relations of the *Cratylus* to Platonism, I shall be altogether on my own ground, as I hope to be able to determine the place which the dialogue occupies in the cycle of Plato's writings, and thus to add something to results which I have already published in a series of papers upon the development of his philosophical system.

The two philosophies come into conflict over three matters : the origin and the significance of names, the false proposition, and, knowledge. About all three controversies something must now be said.

First, of nomenclature. On the strength of Plato's evidence in this dialogue, we are, I think, warranted in supposing that, according to the Heracleiteans, names had their rightness by nature and not by convention, so that names properly so called carried in their etymologies a description of the things named : and further that they tried to escape from the obvious difficulties of this theory by saying that appellations which were not descriptive of the things with which they were associated were not names. It is, I think, also clear that for a justification of this last dogma they relied upon the analogy of the false proposition, which they supposed to be non-significant. I gather further that they had no hypothesis to explain how primary names were invented, and that their theory of names was very far from complete.

On the other hand, Plato's theory of the origin and the significance of names is, at any rate, a serious, sober, reasoned, speculation. I do not know what philologists think of his explanation of root sounds: but, in my ignorance, I have sometimes fancied that he had hit upon, not indeed the whole truth, but a part of it. Whilst however the theory of names was offered as a solid contribution to knowledge, the etymological illustrations were meant to be as farcical as indeed they are. The whole tenor of the exposition proves it. The facility with which etymologies are extemporized; Socrates' surprise at his own proficiency; his alternative solutions; the audacity—no, the impudence, —of his conjectures,—let me remind you that he derives the two genitives of Ζεύς, Διός and Ζηνός from δι' ὃν ζῆν, 'through whom is life,' ἄνθρωπος, 'man,' from ἀναθρεῖ ὃ ὄπωπε, 'he observes what he has seen,' and ἐνιαυτός and ἔτος, 'year,' from ἐν αὐτῷ ἐξετάζον, because 'the year in its course tests the value of its crops';—the inspiration derived from Euthyphro, a wooden, self-righteous, egotistical, prig, who is gibbeted to all time in another dialogue;—all these things indicate that Plato sets no store by the whimsicalities which he pours out. Then again at 406 c he expressly speaks of his efforts as 'playful,' and at 426 B he characterizes his equations of particular sounds with particular actions as 'riotous and ridiculous.' And there are other passages which I might adduce, if this were the proper place for details. But, above all these considerations there is one which seems to me decisive. Plato's argument requires that the etymologies offered should be fanciful. His contention is that the meaning of the name-giver, such as that meaning was, is disguised, destroyed, perverted, by additions, subtractions, substitutions. Now, if he had believed in his etymologies, they would have been so many instances to rebut this contention. In truth, whilst he recognized that in making names men start from names already in use, he had little faith in philological retrospects; and I very much fear that he would have mistrusted some of the results of modern philological inquiry. But perhaps I am doing him a wrong: for he was a man of an open mind.

The theory of the false proposition plays only a subordinate part in the conversation. Forced to acknowledge that there are some appellations which do not describe, Cratylus refuses to call them names: they are, he thinks, empty sounds: and, in justification of this view, he compares the non-descriptive appellation to the false proposition which he supposes to be non-significant. It may seem strange that serious thinkers should have been under any delusion in such a matter: but we must always remember that in the four hundreds the Greeks had very little logic, and that that little was all of it very bad. Seemingly in this particular matter Plato was never in any perplexity: but even Plato did not see his way through another logical puzzle, the paradox of relation, until he had sown his philosophical wild oats.

I come next to the theory of knowledge. At 435 D, where the distinctively philosophical inquiry begins, we learn for the first time the real significance of the

Heracleitean theory of names. Thus far we know only that, according to Cratylus, a name properly so called carries in its etymology a description of the thing signified. We now find that, whereas he is not prepared to trust the testimony of the senses, he is willing to accept the etymological analysis of the name as evidence of the nature or reality of the thing. Probably he thought that, whereas the impressions of sense are transient, mutable, particular, the name represents that which is permanent, stable, general. Possibly he fancied that, in thus relying upon the etymological analysis of names, he was obeying his master's injunctions : ξὺν νόῳ λέγοντας ἰσχυρίζεσθαι χρὴ τῷ ξυνῷ πάντων—'if you would speak with understanding, you must in all things insist upon that which is general,' and τοῦ λόγου ἐόντος ξυνοῦ ζώουσιν οἱ πολλοὶ ὡς ἰδίην ἔχοντες φρόνησιν—'whereas reason is general, most men behave as though they had each a separate intelligence.' It appears further from the concluding sentences of the dialogue that Cratylus used his theory of knowledge to justify his conviction of the universality of flux. Such is the theory of knowledge to which Plato opposed his theory of eternal, immutable, unities, called ideas.

Hitherto, in speaking of these three Heracleitean philosophemes, I have been content to ascribe them to Cratylus. That they were entertained by him, is proved abundantly by my text. But did they originate with him in the late four hundreds ? or did he inherit them from Heracleitus himself, the man of the previous century ? On reflection I think that they cannot go back to the time of the old Ephesian. Let us consider them severally. It is true that Heracleitus propounds some hazardous etymologies : but it is a long step from these occasional escapades to the sweeping declaration—'All names have their rightness by nature and not by convention.' Again, the men of the five hundreds had not begun to trouble their heads about logic, and were not in a position either to conceive or to misconceive the false proposition. Indeed it was not before 470 that the Eleatic Zeno began to puzzle himself and others with certain paradoxes of logic, and I can see no reason for imagining that any one had anticipated his perverse but fruitful ingenuity. Nor can I believe that Heracleitus saw in etymology the one road to the discovery of truth. He may have appealed to names in illustration or justification of his opinions. Indeed it is said that he derived ζῆν 'to live' from ζεῖν 'to boil,' and saw in this etymology a confirmation of his choice of fire to be the fundamental principle ; and in a fragment which I have already quoted, he seems to connect ξυνῷ, 'general' as opposed to 'particular' with ξὺν νῷ, 'with understanding.' It is possible that he saw in names, as Aristotle saw in proverbs, records of the results of experience. But I can hardly think that he was so far in advance of his time as to propound the dogma 'Things may be known through their names and in no other way.' He is, no doubt, a great figure in the history of thought, inasmuch as the theory of flux gave a new set to speculation, and suggested the question 'What is Knowledge?' But asking the question is one thing ; answering it, however ill, is another : and I doubt whether the man of sombre humour, sententious maxims, and mystical phrases—the Heracleitus whom we know in the fragments—could have conceived such a solution. Moreover, if he had offered it, it must needs have left its mark upon the thought of the four hundreds: and it has not done so. Finally, it is to be observed that Plato never makes Heracleitus personally responsible for the doctrine, and that Aristotle, in the passage which I have quoted and in another to the same effect, is equally cautious. For these reasons I am inclined to think that the three Heracleitean theories which Plato criticizes in the body of the dialogue are to be attributed, not to Heracleitus, but to Cratylus: and consequently that the neo-Heracleiteanism of Cratylus ought to have, what at present is not conceded to it, a distinct place in the history of Greek thought.

And now I pass to the question which remains—' How does the *Cratylus* bear upon Platonism?' As we have seen, the dialogue concludes with a declaration that, inasmuch as sensibles are in perpetual flux and therefore unknowable, if there is any knowledge, there must needs be existences other than sensibles to be its objects: and Aristotle assures us that this proposition was the very foundation of the theory of ideas. Plainly this is in some sort an answer to my question. But the theory of ideas appears in many dialogues, and there are obvious diversities in their presentation of it. This being so, it is necessary to ascertain what stage in the development of the doctrine our dialogue represents, and with what other dialogues it is to be associated.

Of all who have occupied themselves with philosophy, Plato seems to have been the most progressive. For myself, I find it necessary to distinguish in his writings five successive phases :

First, in his Socratic period, Plato is content like his master to aim at the more exact definition of ethical terms with a view to greater consistency in conduct.

Secondly, striking out a line for himself, he proceeds to criticize contemporary theories of education, and, incidentally, recognizes certain really existent unities—the self-beautiful, the self-good, and others. That is to say, whereas we perpetually refer beautiful things to what, after him, we still call an 'ideal' standard, and on the strength of the reference pronounce them unbeautiful in this or that respect, Plato conceives the ideal standard, which is eternal, immutable, perfect, to be the sole reality, whereof perishable, mutable, imperfect, beauties are, in the language of Goethe, no more than "likenesses." This is the rudiment, but only the rudiment, of the theory of ideas. At present no attempt is made to determine the content of the world of real existences, or to explain the particular's participation in the idea. To this period belong the *Phaedrus* and the *symposium*.

Thirdly, he develops the rudimentary conception of eternally existent unities into a system capable of affording answers to the three great questions—' What is Being ? ' ' What is Knowledge ? ' ' What is Predication ? ': and in view of the last of the three, he now adds to the fundamental assumption two supplementary articles; first, wherever there is a common term there is an idea, secondly, this idea is present or immanent in each particular. To this period, the period of the earlier theory of ideas, belong the *republic* and the *Phaedo*.

Fourthly, in a group of six dialogues culminating in the great dialogue called *Timaeus* for which my friend Mr Archer Hind has done so much, Plato criticizes his earlier theory, clears up without the aid of the theory of ideas the logical difficulties which had determined the subordinate articles of the previous period, and reconstitutes his system. He now postulates ideas of the cosmos, the heavenly bodies, the four elements, of animal and vegetable species, and of nothing else : each such idea is now a thought of universal mind, and the particulars are imitations of it in matter. In this period it is no longer supposed that men can attain to the direct knowledge of the ideas. Like the mysterious "mothers" of the Second Part of *Faust*, they are divinities enthroned in loneliness, having about them neither space nor time, indescribable : but their existence is, according to Plato, an assurance that there are natural kinds which may be studied scientifically with a view to the discovery of their resemblances and their differences. This is the later theory of ideas.

In the fifth period, that of the *laws*, Plato reverts to the moral and social problems which had occupied his thoughts in middle life, and propounds an elaborate scheme of legislation.

To which of these periods then, does the *Cratylus* belong ? Not to the first, which is pre-metaphysical ; nor to the last which is post-metaphysical. Not to the second, the period of the *Phaedrus* and the *symposium* : for in those dialogues Plato comes to the conception of immutable and perfect unities from the point of view of ethics and aesthetics, and has as yet no thought of them as the objects of knowledge, whereas the immutable and perfect unities of the *Cratylus* are postulated simply and solely that knowledge may be possible. Not to the fourth period, in which, assuming that the fundamental proposition of his theory no longer needs to be justified, Plato reconstitutes his subordinate articles, and in particular retracts his previous recognition of ideas of qualities and the products of art: for in the *Cratylus* the fundamental proposition is announced as a novelty, and the only unities named, the shuttle, the beautiful, the good, are, one of them a product of art, and the other two, qualities.

It only remains to suppose that the *Cratylus* belongs to the third period, the period of the *republic* and the *Phaedo*: and when we bring it into juxtaposition with those dialogues, the harmony is complete. In all three, ideas of qualities are prominent, but there are ideas also of substances: and in all three the ideas are the objects, the sole objects, of knowledge. And I think that we may go a step further and say, not only that the *Cratylus* belongs to the same period as the *republic* and the *Phaedo*, but also that, in the order of thought, it precedes them. For the *Cratylus* enforces the fundamental proposition, and has no reference to the two supplementary articles, whereas the *republic* and the *Phaedo* develop, each of them, one of the two supplementary articles, and take the fundamental proposition for granted. In a word, the *Cratylus*, the *republic*, and the *Phaedo*, seem to me to mark the central point in Plato's intellectual development. Hitherto, he has been an educator with philosophical proclivities : in these dialogues he declares for philosophy : and in the succeeding period, the period of the six dialogues, he writes as a philosopher for philosophers.

In further proof that the *Cratylus* belongs to the same period as the *republic* and the *Phaedo*, I may appeal to a passage in the *sophist*, 248 D. Here, frankly criticizing himself, Plato remarks that, according to his earlier doctrine, soul knows, existence is known : and the tenour of the passage suggests that he has in his eye some previous pronouncement to this effect. We have exactly such a pronouncement in the *Cratylus* at 440 B : and, as the early doctrine criticized in the *sophist* is demonstrably the doctrine of the *Phaedo*, it follows that the *Cratylus* must be ranked with that dialogue and its fellow, the *republic*.

In conclusion, Mr Vice-Chancellor, permit me to say a few words in reply to a reproach which may conceivably be urged, primarily against Plato, secondarily, in so far as I am a student of his writings, against myself. How is it, it may not unfairly be asked,— how is it, that, if Plato was a great philosopher, there can be doubt about the interpretation of his writings ? and if there is doubt about the interpretation of his writings, is it worth while to spend time and trouble upon them ? I am glad to have an opportunity of speaking, however briefly, to these two questions.

Three principal causes have contributed to make a mystery of Plato's teaching. In the first place, he wrote, not so much records for posterity, as rather exercises for his pupils : and, holding with Socrates that the teacher should elicit and suggest rather than inculcate and dogmatize, he was careful always so to frame those exercises that they should stimulate thought and require from the reader an earnest and a conscious effort. Thus in the earlier dialogues he prepares the way for definitions, but refrains from formulating them : and in the later, the conversational form tasks the best energies of a serious student ; and when that student has mastered the dialogue before him, it still remains to coordinate it with others. In fact, like the god of the farmer in Virgil, Plato 'did not mean the road to be easy.'

Secondly, metaphysic was, as has been well said, no more than a brief interlude in the history of Greek thought. It began with Plato, and it ended with Plato. His nephew Speusippus, who succeeded him as head of the Academy, was a biologist who cared for none of these things, and did not even trouble himself about the foundations of his own science. Xenocrates, who followed Speusippus, was an amiable moralist who, out of piety, taught Plato's philosophy, but did not understand it. Then came other moralists, and after them epistemologists sceptically inclined. Thus within the school there was no one to preserve an intelligent tradition. It is true that Aristotle, who, had he been at Athens when Speusippus died in 339, might have succeeded him as scholarch, had a better understanding of Plato : but, not unnaturally, he was more careful to explain his dissent from his master's teaching than to record or interpret it. We have then very little help from tradition.

Thirdly, as I have already said, Plato was beyond all other thinkers progressive, and his writings represent different phases of his intellectual development. There are indeed some who deny the progression: but they are reduced to strange shifts. Either they reject certain important dialogues as spurious, or they set them aside as mere dialectical exercises, or perhaps they fall back upon the dictum which the late Dr Jowett thought conclusive against myself—" We must not intrude upon Plato either a system or a technical language." The sure testimony of Aristotle is decisive against such evasions. If then, as appears, Plato's system grew under his hand, it becomes necessary for us to ascertain the sequence of his writings, and unluckily the external evidence is wholly insufficient for the purpose. These three things, the peculiarity of Plato's exposition, the failure of tradition, and our ignorance about the order of his writings, adequately explain how it is that there is a mystery about Plato's teaching. That the mystery is *not* inexplicable, I am convinced.

In answer to the other question, ' If there is doubt about the interpretation of Plato's writings, is it worth while to spend time and trouble upon them?', I can speak only for myself. Most certainly I do not repent time and trouble given to the study of Plato. For he speaks to me in more ways than one. I am a student of Greek literature: and in my opinion, of all who have used that wonderful instrument, that instrument of many strings, the prose of Athens in the three hundreds, I know of none who can take precedence of him. Again, from early years it has been my business to teach, I like teaching, I have no desire to cease to teach: and, as teacher, I recognize in the *republic,* as Jean Jacques Rousseau did, "the finest treatise on education ever written." Then again, wholly apart from philosophy strictly so called, Plato was interested in questions which from his time to our own were in abeyance, and have come up again within our own memories, questions about the consequences of over-population, about the effect of the healing art upon the race, about the use and the abuse of athletics, about social privileges and limitations, about the severities of war, and the like ; and in dealing with them he seems to me, always original, always judicious, always suggestive. Finally, though to most men of my time metaphysical truth is an aspiration rather than an end, Plato in his later years propounded a scheme to explain the unity of our manifold cosmos, which seems to me even now to deserve consideration. In a word, if Socrates is the master of those who teach, and Aristotle the master of those who know, then Plato is the master of those who think.

Mr Vice-Chancellor and Members of the Senate, my task is done. I am aware that to many of my hearers my theme may have seemed uninteresting, and, possibly, unimportant : and I beg leave to make my apologies. My excuse is that for many years the study of the development of Greek thought has been my professional hobby ; and that I have thought it proper, on this occasion, to bring before the Senate results obtained, but not yet published, in the subject which, both in teaching and in writing, I have tried to make in an especial sense my own. For myself, my faith is that no inquiry is uninteresting, or unimportant, or in any way unworthy, provided that it is pursued methodically and with a view to the discovery of truth.

JAMES ADAM

*THE DOCTRINE OF THE
CELESTIAL ORIGIN OF THE SOUL
FROM PINDAR TO PLATO*

THE DOCTRINE OF THE
CELESTIAL ORIGIN OF THE SOUL
FROM PINDAR TO PLATO.

καὶ σῶμα μὲν πάντων ἕπεται θανάτῳ περισθενεῖ,
ζωὸν δ' ἔτι λείπεται αἰῶνος εἴδωλον· τὸ γάρ ἐστι μόνον
ἐκ θεῶν· εὕδει δὲ πρασσόντων μελέων, ἀτὰρ εὑδόντεσσιν
ἐν πολλοῖς ὀνείροις
δείκνυσι τερπνῶν ἐφέρποισαν χαλεπῶν τε κρίσιν.

PINDAR, *fragment* 131 Bergk.

The body of all men is subject to all-powerful death,
but alive there yet remains an image of the living
man; for that alone is
from the gods. It sleeps when the limbs are active,
but to them that sleep in many a dream
it revealeth an award of joy or sorrow drawing near.

I propose in the present lecture to invite your attention to part of a remarkable fragment of Pindar's dirges, preserved by Plutarch in his *Consolatio ad Apollonium*[1]. It has long been recognised that the Pindaric dirges introduce us to a circle of ideas to which Greek poetry is hitherto a stranger, although parallels are to be found in Orphic eschatology and to a certain extent also in the fragments of Heraclitus. From whatever source

[1] c. 35.

Pindar may have derived his conception of the future world, and he certainly did not evolve it out of his inner consciousness and nothing else, the power of poetry to refine and purify religious sentiment has never been better illustrated than by the poet who throughout his whole career believed himself the chosen servant of Apollo, the god of religious and prophetical as well as of poetical inspiration. My object, however, is not to discuss the origin of these beliefs: it is rather to trace from Pindar to Plato the gradual development and progressive intellectualisation of one of the beliefs contained in the particular fragment which I have put into your hands, and incidentally, perhaps, to remark upon its significance in connexion with later developments in Poetry, Philosophy, and Religion.

A word or two is necessary with reference to the translation. αἰών, which I have taken as 'the living man,' means simply 'life.' Pindar is using the abstract for the concrete. In my opinion Christ is grievously wrong when he explains the word by *aevi sempiterni*, 'eternity': αἰών is never so used by Pindar. In the last line κρίσιν means 'adjudication,' as κρίνω in a passage of the *Pythians* means 'adjudge[1]':

τοῖς οὔτε νόστος ὁμῶς
ἔπαλπνος ἐν Πυθιάδι κρίθη:

'To them, at the Pythian festival, no such glad return to home was adjudged':

but the specific reference in our fragment, as Boeckh and other editors have pointed out, is doubtless to the adjudication of joy and sorrow at the judgment of the

----

[1] 8. 83.

dead. Pindar recognises such a judgment in the second Olympian[1], and implicitly also in other fragments of his θρῆνοι[2] describing the bliss that awaits the pious, and the torments in store for the wicked. Anyone who reads the fragments of the θρῆνοι side by side will agree, I think, that κρίσιν is to be understood in this way.

Let us now turn our attention to the ideas which Pindar's words embody. We note to begin with the survival of the old Homeric notion of the soul as the shadow of the living self. The soul of Patroclus, you remember, appeared to Achilles in a vision of the night, 'in all things like to the man himself, in stature and fair eyes and voice, and the raiment on his body was the same[3].' So far, therefore, we are entirely on Homeric ground. But the rest of the passage belongs to a stratum of ideas which is unlike anything to be found in the *Iliad* or *Odyssey*. In the first place, the soul is said to be of divine descent; secondly, this kinship with the gods is cited as a ground for believing in immortality—τὸ γάρ ἐστι μόνον ἐκ θεῶν, the first indication, I believe, in Greek literature of a definite argument for this belief, such as Plato afterwards developed in the *Phaedo*; and thirdly, the fundamental idea in the last two lines, the idea of which the premonitory vision of the day of judgment is one particular application, is that during life, so long as we are awake and conscious, the soul is asleep, but when the body is laid to rest, the soul awakes and reveals to us in visions of the night that which in our waking moments we cannot see. It is the first of these conceptions, that of the

---

[1] 2. 59.   [2] 130, 132, 133 Bergk.   [3] *Il.* 23. 66.

celestial origin of the soul, with whose development in Greek literature down to Plato I wish at present to deal; but we shall find that the other two ideas are closely bound up with it, and sometimes make their appearance in writers by whom the soul's divinity is affirmed.

In Pindar, as in Heraclitus, a thinker with whom the poet has other points in common besides obscurity, the celestial origin of the soul is still, what it primarily was, a predominantly religious belief; but the germs of a philosophical interpretation are already discernible when the poet deliberately founds his faith in immortality upon this doctrine, and also when by means of it he explains the possibility of divination during sleep. The particular idea involved in the latter part of the passage before us, reappears not only in the *Republic* of Plato[1] but also in an Aristotelian fragment, where we are told that 'whenever the soul is alone and by itself in sleep, it recovers its proper nature,' that is, of course, its celestial nature, 'and divines and prophesies the future[2]'; and the same idea lies at the root of the Stoic philosophy of divination. Nor is it, indeed, unknown in modern psychological thought. Pindar's description of the soul in this passage bears an obvious and striking resemblance to Mr Myers' theory of the subconscious or subliminal self, which, according to the hypothesis of Professor James, is the medium of communication between the soul and that higher or transcendental region which he calls God: nor did the analogy escape Mr Myers, for he chooses the Pindaric fragment as the heading of his chapter on Sleep[3].

[1] IX 572 A.   [2] *frag.* 12.   [3] *Human Personality*, Vol. I p. 121.

In his Ingersoll lecture, again, Professor James makes
the existence of this subliminal self the basis of an
argument for immortality, precisely as Pindar says :
'for this alone is from the gods.' The possibility of
a philosophical development of the Pindaric notion is
also, I think, involved in another passage of Pindar.
You will observe that here it is simply ψυχή—soul in
the old Homeric sense, or not much more—that comes
from the gods. In the sixth Nemean, however, after
emphatically proclaiming the original unity of men and
gods—ἓν ἀνδρῶν, ἓν θεῶν γένος[1]—Pindar suggests that
perhaps the point in which we resemble the immortals
is in *mind* or *reason* (μέγαν νόον)[2]. And it is on the
divinity of νοῦς, rather than of ψυχή, that Greek
philosophy, as we shall presently see, chiefly insists.
This, and not simply the soul or ψυχή, is the philosophical version of that διόσδοτος ἀρχά, that god-given
seed or germ of life which Pindar mentions in yet
another fragment[3]. It would be absurd, of course, to
attribute to a poet any rigid psychological nomenclature;
but no one denies that νοῦς in Pindar is predominantly,
though not exclusively, an intellectual faculty[4]; and in
Greek philosophy itself, even, I believe, in Stoicism,
νοῦς is never the merely *siccum lumen*, the clear, cold
light, which *we* are sometimes in the habit of calling
reason. The dry soul, says Heraclitus, is the wisest :
αὔη ξηρὴ ψυχὴ σοφωτάτη : but, we must remember, it
was made of fire.

---

[1] 6. 1. I agree with Professor Bury in his explanation of these words.
[2] ib. 5.
[3] 137 Bergk.
[4] Διός τοι νόος μέγας κυβερνᾷ, etc., *Pyth.* 5. 122 ; πάντα ἴσαντι νόῳ, ib. 3.
29. See Buchholz, *Sittliche Weltanschauung d. Pind. u. Aesch.* p. 24.

In classical Greek lyric poetry, other than Pindar, there is no certain trace of the ideas we are now considering. The younger Melanippides, who died perhaps about 413 B.C., has left a striking fragment of a prayer, addressed presumably to Dionysus[1]:

κλῦθί μοι, ὦ πάτερ,
θαῦμα βροτῶν, τᾶς ἀειζώου
μεδέων ψυχᾶς.

'Hear me, O Father, honoured of mortal men,
thou that art lord of the ever-living soul.'

If the whole of this poem had survived, it is possible that some further light would be thrown on the subject of this lecture. Aeschylus has one or two definite suggestions of the divine affinity of the soul, notably in the passage where he speaks of the mind's eye as seeing clearly during sleep, whereas in the day men see not the future:

εὔδουσα γὰρ φρὴν ὄμμασιν λαμπρύνεται,
ἐν ἡμέρᾳ δὲ μοῖρ' ἀπρόσκοπος βροτῶν[2].

The notion underlying this passage, and I think also another passage in the *Agamemnon*[3], is the same as we have already found in the fragments of Pindar and Aristotle. In sleep the soul is to a certain extent released from the shackles of the body, and foresees the future by virtue of her natural affinity with the gods. In harmony with this conception, Aeschylus attaches great weight to revelation by means of dreams; and even when the body is awake, in moments of

---

[1] *frag.* 6 Bergk. [2] *Eum.* 104 f.
[3] 189 ff. στάζει δ' ἔν θ' ὕπνῳ κτλ. See Headlam in *Cl. Rev.* for 1903, p. 241.

ecstatic elevation, such as he portrays in the person of
Cassandra, and in those dim forebodings of futurity
that so often haunt the mind of the Chorus in the
Oresteia, the soul appears to give proof of her connexion
with the divine. Nowhere in Aeschylus, however, is
this doctrine brought into relationship with the belief
in immortality, as it is by Pindar; nor, indeed, except
in recognising a judgment and punishments—never, I
believe, rewards—hereafter, and in one or two further
details, do the eschatological pictures of Aeschylus
differ very much from those in Homer, except that
the all-pervading gloom is deeper and more intense.
With regard to Sophocles, I will only say that although
Dronke has rightly called attention to certain exquisite
touches of religious mysticism in his plays, for example
ἀντὶ μυρίων μίαν ψυχήν¹, the particular subject we are
now discussing cannot be illustrated from him. With
Euripides the case is different, and we shall find that
the form in which he expresses the idea of the soul's
divinity is of the highest interest and importance in
connexion with later philosophical thought in Greece.
But before we speak of Euripides himself, it is necessary
to say something about the sources of that distinctive
type of theology with which in his plays and fragments
the notion of man's relationship to God is associated.

In the age of Euripides, the concept of a creative
or world-forming *Nous* or Reason had been made
familiar to Greek thought by Anaxagoras' epoch-making
declaration, πάντα χρήματα ἦν ὁμοῦ· εἶτα νοῦς ἐλθὼν
αὐτὰ διεκόσμησε²: 'when all things were together,

---

¹ *O.C.* 498.   ² ap. Diog. Laert. II 6.

Reason came and set them in order.' Whether the creative νοῦς of Anaxagoras was a purely incorporeal or as we should say spiritual substance or not, is a question still debated; but this much at least is clear, that if it was corporeal, the material of which it was composed differed so much from every other kind of matter that it did not deserve to be called matter at all. To call it by the question-begging epithet of 'thought-matter' or 'thought-stuff,' as Windelband does, throws no light upon its nature, besides being in my judgment a forced and unnatural translation of the Greek word νοῦς. Gomperz talks vaguely of 'a kind of fluid or aether,' a 'curious reasoning fluid,' 'of an extremely refined and mobile materiality[1].' Every such suggestion appears to me incompatible with the well-known criticism in the *Phaedo*, where Plato characteristically blames Anaxagoras, because after announcing that Mind is the cause of everything, he made little or no use of this great principle in explaining the constitution of the Universe, but had recourse to 'airs and aethers and waters and many other such absurdities[2].' The opposition in this passage between *Nous* on the one hand, and the 'airs and aethers' on the other, tells strongly against the identification of *Nous* with any substance of the kind; and, indeed, according to Anaxagoras himself, air and aether are among the substances which *Nous* originally separated off from the primeval mixture or chaos[3]. It is impossible fully to discuss the matter here: I will only say that I agree

---

[1] *Greek Thinkers* (E.T.), I 216, 217.

[2] *Phaedo* 98 C.

[3] *frag.* 2 Diels (*Fragmente der Vorsokratiker*).

with Heinze[1] and Arleth[2] in holding that Anaxagoras probably intended us to understand by *Nous* an incorporeal essence, although in the absence of an accepted philosophical terminology he failed to make the new idea absolutely clear. There are still two points in connexion with Anaxagoras' theory of which my subject requires me to remind you. The world-ordering Reason which he describes is transcendent rather than immanent, although its immanence in certain things is not denied: ἔστιν οἷσι δὲ καὶ νοῦς ἔνι[3]. And finally, although this *Nous* possesses many of the attributes and discharges many of the functions which later philosophy ascribed to the Deity, Anaxagoras in his extant fragments nowhere calls it God.

Turn now for a little to the fragments of Diogenes of Apollonia, who lived in Athens during the latter part of the fifth century B.C., and whose philosophy is in effect little more than a revision of the physical theory of Anaximenes in the light of Anaxagoras' theory of Mind. The primary substance, says Diogenes, of which all other things are only particular forms or differentiations, is 'great and strong and eternal and immortal and possessed of much knowledge' (πολλὰ εἰδός ἐστι)[4], being able 'to preserve the measures of all things, winter and summer, night and day, rains and winds and sunny weather[5].' 'By means of Air,' he says in another fragment, 'all are steered and over all Air has power. For this very thing seems to me God'

[1] *Ueber d.* Noῦs *d. Anaxagoras* (Leipzig, 1890).
[2] *Archiv f. Gesch. d. Philos.* VIII 461 ff.
[3] *frag.* 11 Diels.
[4] *frag.* 8 Diels.
[5] *frag.* 3 Diels.

(αὐτὸ γάρ μοι τοῦτο θεὸς δοκεῖ εἶναι)[1], 'and I believe that it reaches to everything and disposes everything and is present in everything.... There are many forms of living creatures many in number, resembling one another neither in appearance nor in way of life nor in intelligence owing to the multitude of differentiations ; but yet they all live and see and hear by virtue of the same element, and all of them too derive their intelligence from the same source[2].' The Air within us, that is, our reason, Diogenes called a 'little part of God' (μικρὸν μόριον τοῦ θεοῦ)[3]. From these extracts you will see in the first place that Diogenes materializes the νοῦς of Anaxagoras in the element of Air: secondly, that he expressly identifies this noetic Air with God— αὐτὸ γάρ μοι τοῦτο θεὸς δοκεῖ εἶναι : and thirdly, that this divine noetic Air is not transcendent, but only immanent—an all-pervading cosmic Deity, like the λόγος of the Stoics.

I have treated thus briefly of Anaxagoras and Diogenes not so much on their own account, as because of the light which they throw on certain highly characteristic passages of Euripides. The ancients were fond of calling Euripides the 'philosopher upon the stage.' Browning, I think, shews truer insight when he makes him say,

'I incline to poetize philosophy';

and it is with this poetical interpretation of the doctrine of Diogenes that I now proceed to deal. In discussing

---

[1] θεός is Usener's certain emendation for ἔθος.

[2] *frag.* 5.

[3] Diels p. 345. 3.

poetry, more especially dramatic poetry, we must of
course be mindful of Browning's indignant protest,

> 'Which of you did I enable
> Once to slip inside my breast,
> There to catalogue and label
> What I like least, what love best?'

No ancient poet has suffered so much as Euripides
both in his own lifetime and afterwards from the vulgar
species of gallery criticism that hisses the stage-villain.
I may nevertheless be allowed to express my personal
belief that the passages about to be discussed reflect a
tone of feeling peculiarly congenial to the great poet of
humanity, for a reason which will afterwards appear.

Let us now consider some of the passages in
question. We have seen that Diogenes identifies the
all-pervading Air with God. To this theory Euripides
has an allusion in the famous prayer of Hecabe in
the *Troades*[1]:

> ὦ γῆς ὄχημα, κἀπὶ γῆς ἔχων ἕδραν
> ὅστις ποτ' εἶ σύ, δυστόπαστος εἰδέναι,
> Ζεύς, εἴτ' ἀνάγκη φύσεος, εἴτε νοῦς βροτῶν,
> προσηυξάμην σε· πάντα γὰρ δι' ἀψόφου
> βαίνων κελεύθου κατὰ δίκην τὰ θνήτ' ἄγεις:

'O Earth's upholder, throned upon the Earth,' etc.:

for Anaximenes, the philosophical master of Diogenes,
taught that the earth 'rides upon the air' (ἐποχεῖται
τῷ ἀέρι), and also that 'just as our Soul, which is Air,
holds us together, so also breath and Air encompass
the whole Universe[2].' You will remember that Plato,
too, in speaking of this theory, compares the Air to a
βάθρον or pedestal supporting the earth[3]. For the

---

[1] 884 ff.   [2] Diels p. 22 § 6, 25 § 2.   [3] *Phaedo* 99 B.

most part, however, when Euripides writes in this vein, it is Aether and not Air which he calls Zeus. In a poet, of course, we ought not to expect a clear distinction between these two concepts, although Anaxagoras had already differentiated them. Euripides, no doubt, prefers the word 'Aether' partly as having a greater wealth of poetical and religious associations than 'Air.' Thus in one fragment[1] we read

γαῖα μεγίστη καὶ Διὸς Αἰθήρ

'Mightiest Earth and Aether of Zeus';

that is, I believe, not Aether 'home of Zeus,' though Euripides sometimes describes the element in that way, but just 'Zeus's Aether,' the Aether in which Zeus consists, the Aether of which Zeus is made, in no respect different from Zeus himself. The remainder of the fragment clearly shews that Zeus is here identified with Aether. 'Aether,' continues the poet, 'is the father of men and gods ; and Earth receives into her womb the falling rain of dewy drops, and bears mortal men, aye, and food, and the tribes of wild beasts.' But the most characteristic example in Euripides of this identification is contained in the well-known lines :

ὁρᾷς τὸν ὑψοῦ τόνδ' ἄπειρον αἰθέρα
καὶ γῆν πέριξ ἔχονθ' ὑγραῖς ἐν ἀγκάλαις;
τοῦτον νόμιζε Ζῆνα, τόνδ' ἡγοῦ θεόν[2] :

thus translated by Mr Way :

'Seest thou the boundless ether there on high
That folds the earth around with dewy arms?
This deem thou Zeus, this reckon one with God.'

---

[1] 839 Nauck².

[2] *frag.* 941.   Cf. 877 ἀλλ' αἰθὴρ τίκτει σε, κόρα, Ζεὺς ὃς ἀνθρώποις ὀνομάζεται.

There is more than a touch of what W. K. Clifford called 'cosmic emotion' in these verses. Nowhere, however, does ancient literature furnish a more perfect expression of cosmic feeling or a finer example of the poetical treatment of a philosophical conception than we meet with in a less known fragment of Euripides descriptive of the aetherial creative reason indwelling in the world:

> σὲ τὸν αὐτοφυᾶ, τὸν ἐν αἰθερίῳ
> ῥύμβῳ πάντων φύσιν ἐμπλέξανθ',
> ὃν πέρι μὲν φῶς, πέρι δ' ὀρφναία
> νὺξ αἰολόχρως, ἄκριτός τ' ἄστρων
> ὄχλος ἐνδελεχῶς ἀμφιχορεύει[1].

'Thee, self-begotten, who in ether rolled
Ceaselessly round, by mystic links dost bind
The nature of all things, whom veils enfold
Of light, of dark night flecked with gleams of gold,
Of star-hosts dancing round thee without end.'

Mr Way, to whom this translation is due, justly compares the familiar lines of Wordsworth:

'I have felt
A presence that disturbs me with the joy
Of elevated thoughts; a sense sublime
Of something far more deeply interfused,
Whose dwelling is the light of setting suns,
And the round ocean, and the living air,
And the blue sky, and in the mind of man:
A motion and a spirit that impels
All thinking things, all objects of all thought,
And rolls through all things.'

We may say, I think, that in this all-pervading spirit, 'the soul of all the worlds,' as he sometimes calls it, Wordsworth finds the true and essential unity

[1] 593 Nauck[2].

of Nature—it embraces, as Euripides would have said, the 'nature of all things,'

> 'Even as one essence of pervading light
> Shines in the brightest of ten thousand stars
> And the meek worm that feeds her lonely lamp
> Couched in the dewy grass.'

The parallel between Euripides and Wordsworth is here complete; and in Virgil, too, we have exactly the same conception :

> deum namque ire per omnes
> terrasque tractusque maris caelumque profundum[1].

Some may be disposed to call this philosophy, others will call it poetry, and others, perhaps, religion ; but in truth it is only one particular way of trying to express that omnipresent unity which poetry and religion make us feel, which science also presupposes, and which it is perhaps the ultimate goal of a philosophy of the sciences —Plato, at least, believed it was—to demonstrate and apprehend. But to return. I think it is deserving of particular notice that in each of the three poets I have named, this kind of poetical pantheism, or Nature-mysticism, as it may more appropriately be called, is accompanied not only by a deeper sense of the unity between man and nature, but also by a profounder sympathy with 'human weal and woe' than we readily find elsewhere. It was a true instinct that prompted Tennyson to put together in a single stanza these two characteristics of Virgil's poetry :

> 'Thou that seest Universal
>   Nature moved by Universal Mind;
> Thou majestic in thy sadness
>   At the doubtful doom of human kind.'

[1] *Georgics* 4. 221 f.: also in *Aeneid* 6. 724 ff.

The power inherent in Nature dwells also 'in the mind of man,' so that the link which binds us to the one unites us also to the other. You will remember that the later Stoics expressly founded their doctrine of human brotherhood on the presence in all men of the κοινὸς λόγος, or universal reason that 'moves through all things, mingling with the great and lesser lights¹.' Marcus Aurelius, for example, reminds us that man's brotherhood with all mankind depends not on blood, or the generative seed, but on community in mind (νοῦ κοινωνία): each man's mind, he says, is God and an efflux from God²; and God is εἶς διὰ πάντων καὶ οὐσία μία, 'one God, one essence stretching through all things³,' present in Nature as well as in man. The humanism of Euripides is not an intellectual dogma, but the language of the heart; yet it is more than a mere accident—I would rather say it is the operation of a law of nature—that the most profoundly human of tragedians should have been the author of the greatest nature-drama of antiquity, I mean, of course, the *Bacchae*.

So far, I have spoken only of the peculiar kind of poetical theology which is sometimes found in Euripides. That which Pindar calls 'the gods'—τὸ γάρ ἐστι μόνον ἐκ θεῶν—has become, under the influence, perhaps, of Diogenes, an immanent, all-embracing aetherial substance designated by the name of Zeus. Let us now turn from the divine to the human, and consider one or two of those passages in which the poet has in view the doctrine of man's affinity to God. The fragment most

---

¹ Hymn of Cleanthes 12, 13.
² XII 26.   ³ VII 9.

commonly cited by the ancients in this connexion is the
line

ὁ νοῦς γὰρ ἡμῶν ἐστιν ἐν ἑκάστῳ θεός[1].

'The reason in each one of us is God.'

Our first impression is that we have here the same
sentiment as that of Dante, 'Mind is that culminating
and most precious part of the soul, which is Deity[2].'
If we look closer, however, we shall see that the emphasis is on νοῦς and not on θεός: Euripides means
there is no God but reason; and so the line was explained by Nemesius. This is not mysticism, but
rationalism, in the sense in which the word is used
in 'Euripides the rationalist.' In the prayer of Hecabe
it is difficult to say whether the words εἴτε νοῦς βροτῶν
—'Zeus, whether thou art Nature's law or mind of
man'—are meant to be understood in the rationalistic
or in the mystical sense. Perhaps the latter interpretation is the more probable, seeing that Hecabe has
already spoken of Zeus in language suggested by the
theory of Diogenes, according to which the mind of
man is a form of that universally diffused aerial substance which Diogenes holds to be God. I do not
think the two alternatives ἀνάγκη φύσεος and νοῦς
βροτῶν are intended to be rigidly construed; if Zeus,
as Hecabe implies, is omnipresent Air or Aether, he
is at once the law of Nature—an allusion, I think, to
Democritus and the Atomists—and the mind of man.
The real emphasis is on the last line—κατὰ δίκην τὰ
θνήτ᾽ ἄγεις: 'whatever Zeus may be, the sceptre of his
kingdom,' Hecabe means, 'is justice.' But interpret

---

[1] *frag.* 1018.   [2] *Convito* III c. iii p. 143 tr. K. Hillard.

this passage as we may, the doctrine of the kinship between the mind of man and the cosmic mind or aether is clearly involved in two lines of the *Helena*. The speaker is Theonoe, to whose character, as Mr Pearson says, 'an element of mysticism is appropriate.'

ὁ νοῦς
τῶν κατθανόντων ζῇ μὲν οὔ, γνώμην δ' ἔχει
ἀθάνατον, εἰς ἀθάνατον αἰθέρ' ἐμπεσών[1].

'Albeit the mind
Of the dead live not, deathless consciousness
Still hath it, when in deathless aether merged[2].'

Here, of course, we have nothing but a highly philosophized interpretation of the idea underlying the well-known fifth-century epitaph on the Athenians who fell at Potidaea: 'Aether received their souls, and earth their bodies: by the gates of Potidaea they were slain[3].' In the background there is the theory, derived, no doubt, from Anaxagoras, that absolute creation and absolute destruction have no place in the economy of nature; the phenomena we call life and death are only the temporary union and subsequent dissolution of pre-existing and imperishable elements. The bearing of this theory on anthropology is thus expressed by Euripides in a fragment to which I have already referred: 'All things go back whence they came: that which was born of Earth to Earth, and that which sprang from the seed of Aether returns to the firmament of Heaven[4].' You will further notice that in Euripides it is not, as in the epitaph, ψυχή, but νοῦς, that returns to the aetherial element. Elsewhere, in

---

[1] *Hel.* 1014 ff.   [2] Way's translation (substituting 'mind' for 'soul').
[3] *C.I.A.* 1 442.   [4] *frag.* 839.

agreement with Epicharmus (if the fragment is really by Epicharmus[1]), he calls the divine element in man— the element that rejoins the aether—by the name of πνεῦμα,

$$πνεῦμα \ μὲν \ πρὸς \ αἰθέρα$$
$$τὸ \ σῶμα \ δ' \ εἰς \ γῆν^2.$$

It is interesting in this connexion to observe that each of these two terms, νοῦς and πνεῦμα, occupy a somewhat analogous position not only in the psychology of Stoicism, but also in the writings of St Paul, according to whom the highest part of us, the πνεῦμα, 'is what it is by virtue of its affinity to God[3],' 'an element,' as Dr Swete has said, 'corresponding to the Divine Spirit and fitted to be the sphere of His operations[4],' while νοῦς, in the words of another theologian, is in St Paul just 'the πνεῦμα operative as a faculty of knowledge directed toward Divine things[5].' In Euripides, perhaps, it may be doubted whether πνεῦμα really means much more than 'breath'; but νοῦς certainly does, and in this respect there seems to me a real analogy between the Greek and Christian thinker. Still more characteristically philosophical is the distinction which the poet here draws between life and consciousness. The mind, when reabsorbed in aether, no longer lives, that is to say, it has no personal or individual existence, but it nevertheless shares in the consciousness belonging to the universal spirit. The passage we are now discussing is, I believe, the

---

[1] 245, 265 Kaibel.   [2] *Suppl.* 533 f.
[3] Sanday and Headlam, *Romans*, p. 196.
[4] Hastings, *Dictionary of the Bible*, II p. 409 a.
[5] Findlay in Hastings, *l.c.* III p. 720 b.

earliest explicit affirmation in Greek literature of the kind of cosmic immortality which Aristotle ascribes to his νοῦς ποιητικός, and which Marcus Aurelius also had in view when he wrote the words : 'You will disappear in him who gave you being ; or rather you will be changed and reabsorbed into his generative reason' (μᾶλλον δὲ ἀναληφθήσῃ εἰς τὸν λόγον αὐτοῦ τὸν σπερματικὸν κατὰ μεταβολήν)[1]. The ethical and religious value of this conception depends on the extent to which it emphasizes the prospect of reunion with the divine, rather than the consequent extinction of our individuality.   To what heights of almost ecstatic enthusiasm it could sometimes lift the poet may be seen from an extraordinary fragment which would probably have been denounced as a Neoplatonic forgery, if it had not been referred to by Plutarch as well as quoted by Clement : 'Upon my back sprout golden wings : my feet are fitted with the winged sandals of the Sirens : and I shall soar to the aetherial firmament to unite with Zeus'—Ζηνὶ προσμείξων[2]. I think it probable that Zeus in this fragment stands for the ἀθάνατος αἰθήρ with which Euripides elsewhere identifies the god.

In an exhaustive discussion of Euripides' treatment of the subject before us, we should have to take account of many other passages, and particularly of those in which he alludes to the Orphic and Pythagorean view that the body is the prison-house or tomb of the soul : σῶμα σῆμα[3].   But it is preferable, I think, in what remains of my allotted time, to draw your attention, first, to one or two traces of the doctrine of the soul's

---

[1] IV 14.   [2] *frag.* 911.   [3] *fragg.* 638, 833.

divinity in the discourses of the historical Socrates, and afterwards to the part which this doctrine plays in the philosophy of Plato.

The central idea of Socrates' teaching has justly been called Noocracy; what he desired above all things to establish was the rule of Reason alike in the individual and in the state. In like manner, according to Xenophon, he sometimes represented the Godhead as the reason or wisdom indwelling in the world (ἡ ἐν τῷ παντὶ φρόνησις)[1]. No doubt Socrates himself developed the notion on practical rather than theoretical lines, using it as a motive to encourage piety, by dwelling on the unwearied zeal with which this cosmic intelligence consults the interests of man—for his teleology is almost painfully anthropocentric; but there is none the less a real analogy between the Socratic conception and the philosophical theory we have been discussing. And in at least one passage of the *Memorabilia* Socrates definitely suggests that the human mind is itself only a portion of the world-informing Reason, which, according to Xenophon, he occasionally identified with God. Xenophon is relating a conversation between Socrates and Aristodemus, and has reached the point at which the young man, though originally disposed to ridicule the belief in gods, is constrained to allow that there is some little force in the argument from design. 'Well now,' says Socrates, 'do you suppose that you have a little wisdom yourself, and yet that there is no wisdom to be found elsewhere? And that, too, when you know that you have in your body only a small fragment of the mighty earth, and a

[1] *Mem.* I 4. 17.

little portion of the great waters, and of the other elements, extending far and wide, you received, I suppose, a little bit of each towards the framing of your body? Mind alone, forsooth'—*νοῦν δὲ ἄρα μόνον*—adds Socrates, sarcastically, 'which is nowhere to be found, you seem by some lucky chance or other to have snatched up from nowhere[1].' In its full significance, the implication contained in this concluding sentence is that the soul or rather the mind (*νοῦς*) of man is, as the Stoics said, a fragment or *ἀπόσπασμα* of the universal mind or God; but the doctrine is not elsewhere touched upon by the Socrates of the *Memorabilia*, at least in this particular form, although there is one other passage where he pronounces the soul to be divine[2].

The speech of the dying Cyrus in the *Cyropaedia* of Xenophon supplies some additional examples of the type of thought which I am trying to illustrate, and in particular makes the doctrine of the divinity of soul into an argument for immortality and divination. In words that irresistibly recall the *Phaedo* of Plato, Cyrus expresses a disposition to believe that the soul, or rather the *νοῦς* or reason, survives the moment of death, and being then pure and uncontaminated by communion with the body—*ἄκρατος καὶ καθαρός*—attains a measure of intelligence far beyond what it has hitherto enjoyed. When the body dissolves, its component factors, Cyrus says, return to the elements with which they are akin; and what of the soul? We cannot see it as it passes, but neither do we see it while it animates the body. Presumably therefore—this we are left to infer—the soul likewise, in virtue of its divinity, returns to the

---

[1] *Mem.* I 4. 8. [2] See *Mem.* IV 3. 14.

divine. Yet another reason is given by Cyrus for supposing that our intelligence is heightened after death.
In sleep, which is the image and counterpart of death,
the soul most fully realises its kinship with the Godhead, and penetrates the veil that usually hides from us
the future; and the explanation is that during sleep
more than at any other time the soul is freed from the
dominion of the body[1]. For the origin of these and
similar views, which only make explicit what is already
implicit in the fragment of Pindar, we must doubtless
look to the Pythagorean doctrine of the body as the
sepulchre of the soul; but what I wish to suggest is
that it is perfectly possible—for my own part I think it
highly probable—that the historical Socrates sometimes
conversed in this way. The *Cyropaedia* is permeated,
of course, by Socratic ideas; and in this instance the
parallel between Xenophon and Plato is in favour, so
far as it goes, of the presence in their common master
of a similar strain or tendency of thought. Nor are
such ideas otherwise than in harmony with the tem-
perament of Socrates. Although no one ever served
the cause of Reason better, he was not, in any narrow
acceptation of the word, a 'rationalist' pure and simple.
His susceptibility to the influence of dreams, attested
both by Xenophon and Plato; his faith in oracles;
those frequent 'pauses of immobility,' during which he
would stand for hours together, as Gellius says, 'incon-
nivens, immobilis, eisdem in vestigiis, tanquam quodam
secessu mentis atque animi facto a corpore[2]'; and, above
all, the divine sign or 'voice,' the pledge and symbol of
his intimate relationship to God—for these and other

---

[1] *Cyrop.* VIII 7. 19 f. [2] *Noctes Att.* II 1.

features we must seek analogies in the history, not of rationalism, but of religion. It is impossible, I think, to understand the historical Socrates without taking account of the religious as well as of the rationalistic elements in his character; but the link that unites the two is contained in the doctrine that Reason is itself divine: τὸ γάρ ἐστι μόνον ἐκ θεῶν.

From Socrates we now pass to Plato. It would require a treatise to give any adequate idea of the extent to which this doctrine penetrates nearly the whole of Plato's teaching from beginning to end of his long career, and I can hardly even attempt to shew you how, beyond all other Platonic doctrines, it has made Platonism live throughout the ages, not only in poetry, philosophy, and theology, but also, perhaps, in human lives. The most that I can do is to mention one or two different ways in which Plato expresses his belief in man's affinity with the divine, and to indicate a few of the principal implications of the theory in Platonism, with some remarks on its connexion with later religious and philosophical thought.

The nearest analogy in Plato to the kind of cosmic deity of earlier and later Greek philosophy is of course the soul of the world in the *Philebus*[1] and *Timaeus*[2] : but in Plato, I need hardly say, the world-soul differs from the immanent Godhead of Diogenes and the Stoics, inasmuch as it is a purely immaterial or spiritual essence. In the *Philebus* Plato derives the human soul from the soul of the world; and the train of reasoning by which he supports this derivation is only a more developed and expanded form of the argu-

[1] 29 A ff.   [2] 34 C ff.

ment employed by Socrates in his conversation with Aristodemus[1]. But the conception of a cosmic soul, at least in this particular shape, is absent from the earlier dialogues of Plato; and even in the *Timaeus* the human soul, or rather the rational and noetic part of it, is not, as in the *Philebus,* dependent for its origin upon the soul of the world, but, like the world-soul itself, comes directly from the supreme God or Demiurgus. ' As concerning the sovereign part of soul within us,' says Plato, ' that which we say, and say truly, dwells at the top of the body and raises us from earth towards our heavenly kindred, forasmuch as we are a heavenly and not an earthly plant—φυτὸν οὐκ ἔγγειον, ἀλλ' οὐράνιον—we ought to believe that God has given it to each of us as a *daemon*[2],' that is, a genius or guardian angel to direct our lives, in the beautiful phrase of Menander, as it were our μυσταγωγὸς τοῦ βίου[3]. It is in this passage, I believe, that we should seek the origin of the view so much insisted upon by the later Stoics, that the faculty of reason, to quote the words of Marcus Aurelius, is just the δαίμων, ὃν ἑκάστῳ προστάτην καὶ ἡγεμόνα ὁ Ζεὺς ἔδωκεν, ἀπόσπασμα ἑαυτοῦ, ' the genius, which Zeus has bestowed on every man, to be a ruler and guide, even a fragment of himself[4].' In other Platonic dialogues the form of expression is metaphysical rather than theological, though here, too, owing to the characteristically Platonic fusion of theology and metaphysics, there is still a certain colouring of

---

[1] 29 A ff.   [2] *Tim.* 90 A.

[3]   ἅπαντι δαίμων ἀνδρὶ συμπαρίσταται
    εὐθὺς γενομένῳ, μυσταγωγὸς τοῦ βίου.
                    Meineke IV p. 238.

[4] v 27.

theology, or perhaps I had better say, religion. In the *Republic* the soul in its essential, that is, its rational nature, is said to be 'akin to the divine and immortal and ever-existent[1],' that is to the changeless and eternal essence which Plato calls the Ideas; and in the *Phaedo* we read that whenever the soul—and by the soul in this dialogue he means νοῦς—whenever the soul makes use of the body and its senses in any investigation, 'she is dragged by the body into the region of the changeable, and like the objects she is fain to grasp, this way and that she wanders, confused and dizzy like a drunkard. But when she investigates a subject by herself, away she soars into the realm beyond, to join the pure and eternal and immortal and unchangeable, and, *because she is of their kindred*, with them she ever dwells as often as it is permitted her to be alone; and then she no longer wanders, but changes not, because she is in contact with the changeless[2].' You will see from this passage that although the doctrine of the soul's celestial origin has now been intellectualised, its religious meaning is not yet lost. For the nearest parallel to such passages of Plato, and they are very numerous, we must look to the *Paradiso* of Dante. 'Thou shouldest know,' says Beatrice, 'that all have their delight in proportion as their sight sinks deep into that Truth wherein every intellect finds rest[3].'

I say no more at present about the manifold ways in which the infinite variety of Plato's genius gives expression to the old Pindaric sentiment, τὸ γάρ ἐστι μόνον ἐκ θεῶν. Before, however, touching on the applications of the doctrine in Platonism, let me call

[1] 611 E.   [2] 79 C ff.   [3] Canto 28. 106 ff.

your attention to a new and historically fruitful idea
with which Plato enriches this ancient belief. The
question as to the essential meaning of the word man
—what it is in virtue of which we are said to be human
—had hardly as yet been raised by Greek philosophy.
In the view of Plato, it is just the presence of this
divine element that makes us specifically human. Man
is most truly man when he most resembles God. This
suggestion is clearly intended in two passages of the
Republic. The first is where Plato is describing how
the true legislative artist will endeavour to model the
character and lives of men after the image of the divine.
Looking now at natural, that is, ideal—observe how
the natural in Plato is always the ideal—Beauty and
Justice and Temperance, and now at the actual picture
he is painting, he will, says Plato, blend and mingle
institutions, like so many colours, until he has obtained
τὸ ἀνδρείκελον, the colour and complexion of true manhood; and he will found his idea of the ἀνδρείκελον
on that which, when it appears among men, Homer
himself called θεοειδές τε καὶ θεοείκελον[1]. The Man-
like, in short, is the Godlike. The second passage
occurs in the elaborate comparison of human nature as
it now is to a kind of chimaera or triple-headed creature,
wearing the vesture of humanity, and comprising within
its folds a many-headed monster, symbolical of desire,
a lion, symbolical of spirit, and withal what Plato, in
language made familiar to us by St Paul, declares to
be the 'inward man' (ὁ ἐντὸς ἄνθρωπος)[2], in other words

---

[1] ξυμμιγνύντες τε καὶ κεραννύντες ἐκ τῶν ἐπιτηδευμάτων τὸ ἀνδρείκελον,
ἀπ᾽ ἐκείνου τεκμαιρόμενοι, ὃ δὴ καὶ Ὅμηρος ἐκάλεσεν ἐν τοῖς ἀνθρώποις
ἐγγιγνόμενον θεοειδές τε καὶ θεοείκελον *Rep.* 501 B.   [2] 589 A.

the νοῦς or Reason. What account, then, Plato asks, shall we give of virtue? We will say that virtue consists in bringing the bestial elements—the lion and the ape—into subjection to the human, 'or rather,' he adds, 'or rather, shall we say, *to the Divine*' (τῷ ἀνθρώπῳ, μᾶλλον δὲ ἴσως—τῷ θείῳ)[1]. The suggestion that man is truly human just in proportion as he is divine was afterwards taken up by Aristotle and the Stoics[2]; and no one can fail to see its hitherto unexhausted, perhaps for ever inexhaustible, significance in religion. 'It would seem,' says Aristotle, 'that *this*' —meaning the divine or rational part of man—'is actually the self' (δόξειε δ' ἂν καὶ εἶναι ἕκαστος τοῦτο)[3], 'inasmuch as it is the supreme and better part of man.' The implication in the epithet 'better,' that the good alone is the truly existent, is not less Platonic than the pregnant and powerful phrase in which the pupil of Plato points the moral lesson of this and all his master's teaching : ἐφ' ὅσον ἐνδέχεται, ἀθανατίζειν, 'put on the immortal, as far as in thee lies.'

Consider now some of the implications of this theory in Platonism. Since man is by nature akin to the divine, the end and object of his existence must of necessity be ὁμοίωσις τῷ θεῷ, 'assimilation to God' : the fullest possible realisation in this mortal life of that immortal nature which alone can truly be called our own. The doctrine of ὁμοίωσις τῷ θεῷ plays a conspicuous part in the teaching of Plato. 'It is God,' he says in the *Laws*[4], 'and not, as some have asserted,

---

[1] 589 D.
[2] See (for the Stoics) e.g. Marc. Aur. XII 3.
[3] *Eth. Nic.* X 7. 9.   [4] 716 C.

man, who ought to be to us the universal measure or
standard.' This is the dominating motive throughout
nearly the whole of Plato's polemic against Homer in
the second and third books of the *Republic* : the
Homeric gods are to be discarded because they do not
provide a moral ideal for mankind—Euripides, you
remember, had the same idea, and so had Xenophanes
before him : and this is also the principle of the re-
formed theology which Plato is desirous of inaugurating
in his ideal state. In its political application, the ὁμοίωσις
θεῷ means the establishment of a kingdom of righteousness upon earth : for δικαιοσύνη in the *Republic* is not
really a specific virtue, but righteousness, the root and
source of all the individual virtues, the virtue about
which Aristotle[1], quoting a fragment of Euripides[2], says
that 'neither the morning nor the evening star is so
beautiful.' Plato in the *Republic* is looking for a *civitas
dei*—new heavens and a new earth, ἐν οἷς δικαιοσύνη
κατοικεῖ[3] : and indeed, as the argument unfolds itself,
we behold the originally 'Hellenic city' gradually
changing into a celestial commonwealth, a παράδειγμα
ἐν οὐρανῷ, as Plato himself at last confesses it to
be[4].

If we limit our survey to the progress towards per-
fection of the individual man—and in Plato political is
always founded upon private virtue—we may say, I
think, that the realisation by the individual of his true
and immortal nature is described by Plato from three
main points of view. In the *Phaedo* it appears as the
μελέτη θανάτου, the 'study' or rather 'rehearsal of

---

[1] *Eth. Nic.* v 1. 15.   [2] 490 Dindorf: cf. Nauck[2] 486.
[3] 2 Pet. iii 13.   [4] *Rep.* 470 E, 592 B.

death,' the mortification of our lower nature for the
sake of reviving the higher, dying, in short, that we
may live. The germ of this conception is of course
much older than Plato, as he himself points out. I will
quote a single illustration from Heraclitus. 'Both
living and dying are present in our life and in our
death ; for when we live our souls are dead and buried
in us, and when we die our souls revive and live[1].'
And the Orphic and Pythagorean religious discipline
was already to a certain extent a practical illustration
of the Platonic precept. You will observe, however,
that in the fragment of Heraclitus 'we' means rather
the body than the soul, whereas in Plato, as we have
seen, the true personality is the νοῦς : and it is the life
of νοῦς while still imprisoned in the body that the
Platonic 'meditatio mortis' is intended to resuscitate.
The soul of the lover of wisdom, says Plato, 'withholds
herself from pleasures and desires and pains and fears
so far as she is able' ; for she knows that every new
indulgence will add to the chains from which she longs
to be released[2]. We must fly away yonder, far from
the world of sense and sensual things : χρὴ ἐνθένδε
ἐκεῖσε φεύγειν : and the way of flight is to grow like
unto God in righteousness, holiness, and—observe the
characteristic addition—in wisdom[3]. The Platonic
μελέτη θανάτου or 'rehearsal of death' has often been
compared with the Pauline doctrine of *Necrosis*, but
the parallel deserves, I think, an even closer examination than it has yet received. There is hardly any
subject of investigation which invites and permits one
to turn so clear a light upon the points of contrast as

[1] ap. Sext. Emp. *Pyrrh.* III 230.   [2] *Phaedo* 82 C ff.   [3] *Theaet.* 176 B.

well as similarity between Platonic and Pauline thought. One such contrast lies in the predominantly intellectual or rather noetic character of the aspiration expressed in Plato's 'rehearsal of death.' I say predominantly intellectual, for it is by no means exclusively so. What Mr Nettleship has said of Greek philosophy in general is pre-eminently true of Plato. 'We say that Greek moral philosophy, as compared with modern, lays great stress on knowledge and gives excessive importance to intellect. That impression arises mainly from the fact that we are struck by the constant recurrence of intellectual terminology, and omit to notice that reason or intellect is always conceived of as having to do with the good. Reason is to Greek thinkers the very condition of man's having a moral being....Their words for reason and rational cover to a great extent the ground which is covered by words like "spirit," "spiritual," and "ideal" in our philosophy. They would have said that man is a rational being, where we should say that he is a spiritual being[1].' In this way, I believe, the life of Reason, in Plato, becomes not only intellectual, but also something akin to what is afterwards called spiritual life : for in Platonism, as the Cambridge Platonists were fond of saying, it is always Reason which is the 'candle of the Lord.' At the same time the contrast holds good, with the qualification that I have mentioned. A second and closely related point of difference between St Paul's *Necrosis* and Plato's μελέτη θανάτου is to be found in the strain of asceticism in the *Phaedo*, though here again the exercise of νοῦς brings pleasures of its own, the truest and purest

---

[1] *Lectures and Remains*, II p. 221.

pleasures, Plato says; and Gomperz is right in saying
that although *Weltflucht* touched the soul of Plato,
it never enchained it. But the really fundamental
contrast has already been pointed out by Matthew
Arnold[1]. I will venture to put it in a single phrase of
St Paul, a phrase that as if by the touch of some
heavenly alchemy at once transforms a philosophy into
a religion : ἀποθανεῖν σὺν Χριστῷ. λόγον ἔχεις, says
Marcus Aurelius, τί οὖν οὐ χρᾷ ; τούτου γὰρ τὸ ἑαυτοῦ
ποιοῦντος, τί ἄλλο θέλεις[2]; 'thou hast reason : why then
not use it ? If reason does its work, what else dost
thou require ?' St Paul's σὺν Χριστῷ supplies the
something else—the driving power which has made
the Platonic μελέτη θανάτου an inexhaustible source of
moral inspiration throughout the ages.

The second of the two aspects in which Plato
represents this great idea is that which is developed in
the *Symposium* and elsewhere. The object of adoration
in that dialogue is not so much the primal Goodness, as
the primal Beauty, the divine Beauty of which Plato
says that it is ever-existent, alike uncreated and imperishable, knowing neither increase nor decay, beautiful
always and everywhere and in all relations and respects ;
and all other things which we call beautiful are beautiful
because they participate in it, yet in such a way that
although beautiful particulars come into being and
perish, the Ideal Beauty nevertheless suffers no
diminution nor increase nor change of any kind at all[3].
The path of the soul in the *Symposium* leads upwards
from the lovely things of earth to those of heaven ; we

---

[1] *St Paul and Protestantism*, p. 53, ed. 1889.
[2] IV 13.   [3] 211 A, B.

should use the former as ἐπαναβαθμοί or stepping-stones, passing first from one to all fair bodies, next from corporeal beauty to the beauty of institutions and from institutions to sciences, until we arrive at the study of Ideal Beauty, and at last perceive the Beautiful in its true and essential nature[1]. 'Suppose,' concludes Diotima, 'suppose it were granted to one to behold the Beautiful itself, pure and clear and unadulterated, not tainted by human flesh or colours which man has made, or any other of the countless vanities of mortal life, but the Divine beauty as it stands in its simplicity and isolation : do you think it would be an ignoble life that we should gaze thereon and ever contemplate that Beauty and hold communion with it ? Or rather do you not think that in this communion only is it possible for a man, beholding the Beautiful with the organ wherewith alone it can be seen, to beget, not images of virtue but realities, for that with which he holds communion is not an image, but the truth, and having begotten and nourished true virtue to become the friend of God and be immortal, if ever mortal has attained to immortality[2].' The contemplation of the Ideal Beauty is in Plato life—nay more, it is 'eternal life'—ἐνταῦθα τοῦ βίου, εἴπερ που ἄλλοθι, βιωτὸν ἀνθρώπῳ, θεωμένῳ αὐτὸ τὸ καλόν[3]. This is the side of Platonism which has appealed in all ages to the religious mystic, the poet, and the artist. Of its influence in religious mysticism, the Bampton lectures of Mr Inge will supply you with many examples ; in sculpture, its greatest exponent, perhaps, is Michael Angelo, whose sonnets also bear witness to the fervour of his Platonism ; and

[1] 211 B f. [2] 211 D—212 A. [3] 211 D f.

in poetry, the central idea of the *Symposium*, expressed
by one of the Cambridge Platonists in the lines

> 'All streams of Beauty here below
> Do from that immense Ocean flow,
> And thither they should lead again[1]';

in poetry, I say, this great conception inspires the
whole of Dante's *Divine Comedy*, and finds fit utterance
in many single passages of the *Paradiso*. 'The leaves
with which all the garden of the eternal Gardener
blooms, I love in measure of the good transmitted to
them from him[2].' And in another canto : ' Behold now
the height and amplitude of the Eternal Worth, seeing
it hath made itself so many mirrors in which it breaks,
while remaining one in itself, as before[3].' A more
perfect expression of the essential content of Platonism
is not to be found in the writings of Plato himself.

Thirdly, the ascent of the soul towards the fountain
of her being is represented by Plato as an educational
process—the pursuit of knowledge. This is unques-
tionably the most characteristic and fruitful point of
view from which he regards the matter : indeed it is
the point of view which ultimately includes and embraces
all the others. In every human creature, he holds,
there is present from the first an organ whose preserva-
tion is of more importance than a thousand eyes : since
by it alone Truth is seen[4]. This faculty, 'the vision
and the faculty divine,' it is the business of the educator

---

[1] John Norris (quoted by Harrison, *Platonism in English Poetry*,
p. 86).

[2] *Par.* 26. 64 ff. Cf. especially *Il Convito*, IV c. 12.

[3] *Par.* 29. 142.

[4] *Rep.* 527 E.

to nurture and develope, not to instil into his pupils
from without : for

> 'to know
> Rather consists in opening out a way
> By which the imprisoned splendour may escape
> Than in effecting entry for a light
> Supposed to be without.'

The principle enunciated in these lines determines
the whole of Plato's educational method and curriculum.
In earlier years the object is to bring the mind into
unconscious harmony with the beauty of reason through
the influence of Poetry and Art, the proper function
of which, in Plato's way of thinking, is to 'track out
the beautiful'—ἰχνεύειν τὴν τοῦ καλοῦ φύσιν[1]—as it is
manifested in nature, in the human form, and in the
works and characters of men, and embody this and this
alone in the material with which they deal. Later,
when the reasoning powers begin to awaken, the discipline becomes severely intellectual, only such studies
being admitted as are able, in Platonic phrase, to purge
and revivify (ἐκκαθαίρειν τε καὶ ἀναζωπυρεῖν[2]) the eye
of the soul : but Plato is careful to insist that the
rational faculty can never be turned from darkness to
light unless the whole nature of the man is turned
along with it ; and one of the incidental results of the
higher curriculum is to strengthen the moral discipline
of youth by disclosing the bed-rock of reason on
which it was founded. In the truly philosophic nature,
according to Plato, it is the *amor intellectualis*, the
passion for truth, not this or that portion of truth,
but all truth, everywhere and always, that is the

---

[1] *Rep.* 401 C.   [2] *Rep.* 527 D.

source of all the moral virtues too—courage and high-mindedness, temperance, justice, kindness and the rest[1]. In the last analysis, morality, in Plato, is the love of Truth. By the ladder of the mathematical sciences, or as Plato is already beginning to call them, 'arts'—in this originating, as I have elsewhere tried to shew, our modern academic usage of the word—the mind slowly and laboriously climbs upward into the kingdom of realities ; for we must get behind and above mathematics, behind every other single science, if we are really to attain to knowledge, as the word is understood by Plato. To this elevation we rise by what he calls Dialectic, in the view of Plato the science of sciences, above and beyond all other sciences, even as its final object, the Idea of the Good, determines all the other Ideas. If we may try to interpret Plato's dream in something like the language of to-day, and it is a dream which is a little nearer to fulfilment now than in his time, we may say, perhaps, that the ultimate goal of knowledge is not even then attained when each particular science has at last combined and correlated its several classes of phenomena under adequate generalisations and these again under one supreme generalisation which will constitute the ἀρχή or first principle of the science. Something more than this is needed, something like the ideal which a recent writer had in view when he suggested that ' in another age, all the branches of knowledge, whether relating to God or man or nature, will become the knowledge of "the revelation of a single science," and all things, like the stars in heaven, will shed their light upon one another[2].'

[1] *Rep.* 485 A ff. [2] Jowett, *Plato* II p. 25.

The first principles of the several sciences must in their turn be correlated with one another and themselves subsumed under the first principle of all, which in Plato is the Good. It is only then that the philosopher becomes 'a spectator of all time and all existence,' only then that he recognises the essential unity of knowledge and understands in the fullest sense—observe how poetry again comes to the aid of science—understands how

> 'The whole round world is every way
> Bound by gold chains about the feet of God.'

And the weapon to be employed throughout the whole of this enquiry is not the intuitive, but the analytic and discursive intellect, whose province it is by patient and laborious investigation to demonstrate that Unity, in which the intuitive intellect, by reason of its affinity thereto, has always and everywhere found rest.

The dialectic of Plato, like his conception of Good, is an ideal, and as such unattainable, perhaps, οὐ πρακτὸν οὐδὲ κτητὸν ἀνθρώπῳ, Aristotle might have said. Well, it is Plato's way to make us

> 'breathe in worlds
> To which the heaven of heavens is but a veil.'

And if we consider his dialectic simply as an ideal, it is, I venture to think, the kind of ideal for which, apart from idiosyncrasies of thought and language, philosophy is looking still, towards the realisation of which, if we believe in the unity of knowledge, every investigator does his part, in however humble a sphere, whether he studies man or nature, and whether he succeeds or fails, if only he is actuated by the love of truth. It is false to say that such an ideal is useless because it lies beyond our present powers. Some men are so constituted that they need the stimulus of the unattainable to make them reach the utmost limits of that to which they can attain. And in point of fact, an Ideal, as Plato well knew—I believe it to be the meaning of the one great paradox of the Ideal theory—an Ideal is from its very nature immanent as well as transcendent, always being realised in the progress we make towards it. Already we 'know in part': ἐκ μέρους γινώσκομεν[1]. The higher we climb the hill of knowledge in this life, the nearer we come to that transcendent Unity—call it by what name you will, the Absolute, or God, or Nature; for all our names are but a shadow of the Truth—wherein 'are all the treasures of wisdom and knowledge hidden.' But to Plato this life is not all: it is only a single stage upon our journey. The Platonic doctrine of immortality holds out the hope of a continuous advance throughout a series of lives until at last knowledge is made perfect. With perfect knowledge, too, comes perfect goodness or 'assimilation to God'; for knowledge in Plato transforms the moral as well as the intellectual nature, and the Form of Good, which is the source of knowledge, is also the fountain of virtue. And in Plato as in Pindar, the ultimate proof of immortality—the proof that lies deeper than all his arguments and yet is heard throughout them all—is the kinship of the human soul with the divine: τὸ γάρ ἐστι μόνον ἐκ θεῶν.

In the speech delivered by St Paul before the council of the Areopagus, the doctrine which the apostle declares to be the common meeting-ground of Greek

---

[1] 1 Cor. xiii 9.

and Christian thought is just the doctrine which I have tried to explain and illustrate throughout this lecture. 'In him we live and move and have our being; as certain even of your own poets have said, For we are also his offspring': τοῦ γὰρ καὶ γένος ἐσμέν. I have endeavoured to shew you that St Paul might with equal truth have added 'and as certain of your own philosophers have said': and I have tried to put before you what I believe the doctrine really means alike in Poetry and in Philosophy. The all-embracing and yet all-transcending unity, in which 'we live and move and have our being' is just that ultimate reality which Religion, Philosophy and Poetry, each in their own language—remember, ὅστις ποτ᾽ εἶ σύ, δυστόπαστος εἰδέναι—are trying now and always to interpret to the human intellect or heart; and the doctrine of man's relationship to that great unity—τοῦ γὰρ καὶ γένος ἐσμέν—is not the fading echo of a 'dead philosophy': it is still, what Plato made it, the ever-living watchword of idealism.

In conclusion, I would ask you to link the present with the past by adding to the passages I have discussed the not less noble verses of our greatest living poet, himself a scholar in the highest or creative meaning of the word :

> 'Mother of man's time-travelling generations,
> Breath of his nostrils, heart-blood of his heart,
> God above all gods worshipped by all nations,
> Light above light, law beyond law thou art.
> Thy face is as a sword smiting in sunder
> Shadows and chains and dreams and iron things:
> The sea is dumb before thy face, the thunder
> Silent, the skies are narrower than thy wings.

*   *   *   *   *

All old gray histories hiding thy clear features,
O secret spirit and sovereign, all men's tales,
Creeds woven of men thy children and thy creatures
They have woven for vestures of thee and for veils.

Thine hands, without election or exemption,
Feed all men fainting from false peace or strife,
O thou the resurrection and redemption,
The godhead and the manhood and the life[1].'

[1] Swinburne, *Mater triumphalis.*

A. W. VERRALL

THE VOTE OF ATHENA

THE VOTE OF ATHENA.

ἐμὸν τόδ᾽ ἔργον, λοισθίαν κρῖναι δίκην·
ψῆφον δ᾽ Ὀρέστῃ τήνδ᾽ ἐγὼ προσθήσομαι.
μήτηρ γὰρ οὔτις ἐστὶν ἥ μ᾽ ἐγείνατο,
τὸ δ᾽ ἄρσεν αἰνῶ πάντα, πλὴν γάμου τυχεῖν,
ἅπαντι θυμῷ, κάρτα δ᾽ εἰμὶ τοῦ πατρός.
οὕτω γυναικὸς οὐ προτιμήσω μόρον
ἄνδρα κτανούσης δωμάτων ἐπίσκοπον·
νικᾷ δ᾽ Ὀρέστης, κἂν ἰσόψηφος κριθῇ.
AESCHYLUS, Eumenides, 734—741.

In the *Eumenides* of Aeschylus the goddess Athena is represented as founding, for the trial of the matricide Orestes, the court of Areopagus, and introducing, for the first time, the method of trial by jury. When the jury of Athenian citizens have voted, by ballot and secretly, and before the votes are counted, the goddess herself, in the passage which I am specially to consider, gives, or declares her intention to give, a vote on her own behalf. The precise effect of this vote, and its relation to those of the jury, has been the subject of a long and animated controversy, which, in the latest commentaries, is still regarded as open, and rightly to this extent, that no positive proof can be given on either side of the question.

The words of Athena I would translate as follows : ' Here is a task for me, to give a last deciding sentence. And this, *my* vote, I shall reckon to Orestes. For mother is there none who bare me ; but in all things, save to be wedded, I yield with whole heart praise to the masculine, and am verily of the father's side. Therefore I shall not prefer in value the death of a woman, who slew her man, the lawful overseer of the house ; Orestes, even with equal votes, hath the victory.' Whereupon the votes are counted and declared to be equal, and the defendant is dismissed accordingly.

Now the question raised—a question of the first importance to the significance of the scene and play—is this. Does Athena mean that her vote, whether actually put in the urn or supposed to be put, is to be counted with the rest as a judicial vote for acquittal ; and that if, *with this vote*, there is equality, then, by her separate ruling in view of that case, the defendant escapes ? Or, on the other hand, does she simply give such a ruling, and is this, the ruling that, if the votes of the jurymen are equally divided, the defendant escapes, the whole effect of what she calls her vote ? Very good names may be cited for the first view, but the latter is prevalent ; my purpose is to reinforce and extend some arguments for it, which perhaps have not had their full weight.

As acted, the scene must have been clear, either in one sense or in the other. The jurymen are seen to vote ; and from the dialogue, which accompanies their voting, it is plain that they come to the urns in some regular, symmetrical way. Their visible number, odd or even, would show that, as between them only, either there could be equality, or there could not. But the division of that dialogue can be accommodated to either supposition, and we must fall back upon the words of Athena.

To a native ear these also may perhaps have been decisive ; but to us, it must be admitted, they are not. All depends upon the length of a pause, upon the choice between colon and full stop. ' Therefore I shall not prefer in value the death of a woman who slew her man. And, even with equal votes, Orestes hath the victory.' Shall we read so, or shall we read rather thus ?—' Therefore I shall *not* prefer in value the death of a woman who slew her man, but Orestes, even with equal votes, hath the victory.' In νικᾷ δ' Ὀρέστης, is the conjunction δέ merely copulative, adding a fresh point, or is it adversative, making an antithesis between οὐ προτιμήσω, ' I shall not prefer ', and νικᾷ δ' Ὀρέστης, ' but Orestes wins ', as opposite sides of the same fact, the ruling of the goddess upon the case of equality ? To modern judgments such a question, as a mere point of language, seems to present an insoluble ambiguity.

To review the debate, which has ramified through considerable volumes, would be far beyond my limit. For the side which I do not favour, the principal, perhaps the only solid argument is this. The magistrate, who presided at trials before the Areopagus, did in fact vote along with the jurors. So we are told on authority not very high but uncontradicted. In the *Eumenides*, Athena undoubtedly represents in a general way the presiding magistrate. It is assumed, though not stated, that the magistrate voted as a juror, judicially, and on the merits. And it is argued therefore, that Athena must do the same, and her vote must be counted simply as one among the rest, contributing to make a possible equality. Of this I shall say only that neither the assumption appears inevitable, nor the inference that the same procedure must be followed by Aeschylus, when he had placed a goddess in the chair.

On the other side, my own side, the principal stress has been laid upon the solemn declaration of the Aeschylean Athena that she will not be a judge in the case of Orestes, that such an office is unfit for her (*v.* 471). It is expressly on this ground that she places the introduction of the jury. If, after all, she gives a judicial vote on the merits, the only vote for which reasons are stated, and the vote which does in fact decide the judicial issue, her previous declaration is practically cancelled; and we must suppose either that the poet overlooked this inconsistency, or that for some reason he could not avoid it. We might suppose so, but it is not satisfactory.

Minor points on both sides I pass over, and come to that which I specially wish to fortify. It seems generally to be taken for granted, on both parts, that the question is merely one of legal form and the history of Areopagitic procedure; that, whether Athena votes, technically speaking, on the judicial issue, or whether she merely gives a ruling in case of equality between the jurors, she does in fact form an opinion upon the judicial issue, and the words, by which she accompanies her vote, are an expression of that opinion. This being taken for granted, little has been said, so far as I have observed, upon the quality of her reasons, and their value as basis for an opinion upon the merits of Orestes' case. But I submit that this is hardly just to the poet. He could not have professed, consistently with the spirit of his trilogy as a whole, to give in his own words a divine and decisive judgment upon the problem which is submitted to the Areopagus ; and if he had thought fit to do so, he would at all events have provided some other and different reasons from those which he here attributes to Athena.

The problem before the court is briefly this, whether in extreme circumstances a son might be justified who, in revenge for his father, took the life of his mother with his own hand. ' My vote,' says the goddess, ' I shall reckon as added to Orestes. For mother is there none who bare me, but in all things, save to be wedded, I yield with whole heart praise to the masculine, and am verily of the father's side.' Now if this is meant for a superhuman opinion on the merits of the case, a decisive weight in the balance of judgment, the grounds are surely not inadequate merely but offensively irrelevant. It was scarcely worth while to pursue the history of the crime through three tragedies, deepening the mystery and, if I may use a common phrase, piling up the agony on both sides in a series of striking scenes and solemn odes, in order to reach the conclusion, that moral judgment is a personal accident, depending on the casual predilections of the judge. How can it affect the guilt or innocence of Orestes, that Athena, from the circumstances of her origin, is generally predisposed in favour of fathers as against mothers ? Would such a reason have been thought decent, *mutatis mutandis*, for a human judge, for one of the Athenian Areopagites ? The jurymen are solemnly warned, as they respect their oaths, to consider nothing extraneous to the case as sworn before them[1]. Do these warnings mean that an Areopagite, who from a comparison of his own parents had derived a partiality for either sex, was at liberty to indulge this partiality by acquitting or condemning the matricide arraigned before him? Yet why not, if Athena may properly base her opinion of the case on the fact that she had no mother at all?

In saying that Aeschylus, if he had wished to furnish Athena with a judicial opinion, would have provided her with reasons better than this, I do not overlook the possibility that this reason may have been attributed to the goddess by tradition. We have no proof of this; we have no evidence at all that the story of Orestes' trial and Athena's vote had been cast, before Aeschylus, into any such dramatic or other literary form as would require a statement of her reasons. It is at least possible that, before Aeschylus, the whole story was a mere anecdote, supplying a dignified precedent for the practice of Athenian jurycourts, that equality of votes meant acquittal. But suppose otherwise; suppose that a bad and irrelevant

---

[1] See the trial-scene *passim* and also *vv.* 487—489:

κρίνασα δ' ἀστῶν τῶν ἐμῶν τὰ βέλτατα
ἥξω, διαιρεῖν τοῦτο πρᾶγμ' ἐτητύμως,
ὅρκων περῶντας μηδὲν ἔκδικον φρεσίν.

Sic Cod. Med. The last verse, *frustra tentatus*, is correct. The genit. ὅρκων depends upon ἔκδικον; the oaths meant here, as the context shows (*v.* 486), are those of the parties and witnesses, not of the judges; and the literal translation is 'not travelling at all in their thoughts beyond the sworn pleas (δίκαι),' that is to say confining their attention strictly to the case and its merits.

reason, alleged by Athena, was part of the tradition. That would not have bound Aeschylus to adopt it. He has modified and contradicted the tradition in points fully as important as this. He contradicts tradition when he says that the Areopagite court was first introduced for the trial of Orestes. He modifies tradition, and on a vital point, when he makes the jury men. The canonical legend said they were gods, and held to this view, as we see by the references of Athenian orators, always, so far as we know, even after Aeschylus, and in spite of the emphatic disclaimer of such a function, which he, with his more spiritual theology, puts, as we noted before, into Athena's mouth. Innovating as he does, in these and other points, he could have changed Athena's reason for her vote, if he had thought it bad ; and bad he surely must have thought it, if, in his conception, it was to serve as basis for a moral opinion and for a judgment on the case.

But if we take the other alternative, and suppose that the judicial question, the question 'guilty or not guilty?', is really left, as Aeschylus expressly asserts, to the jury and the jury only, and that the question decided by Athena is merely the practical question, what shall be done with an accused person, whom an impartial court, representing the best opinion applicable, neither condemns nor absolves, being equally divided—then it is possible to think that Aeschylus shows both candour and perspicacity in making the decision a mere accident, and not even professing to ground it upon reason at all. For this is what it comes to. The final release of Orestes, he being by the court neither condemned nor absolved, is due to the fact that it is Athena, and not some other person, in whose hands he is thus left, that is, to the fact that he is tried in Athens. *Caeteris paribus*, which parity the trial and division of the court establishes, she acts openly upon her personal inclination. But if the defendant had taken refuge, let us say, in Samos, or had been tried in his native Argos, and a Samian or Argive Areopagus, constituted by the goddess Hera, had divided equally upon his case, then Hera, it would appear, being personally in favour of the feminine side, might have delivered him to the Furies, with no less reason, or lack of it, than Athena has for releasing and protecting him. Οὐ προτιμήσω, says Athena. She will *not prefer* Clytaemnestra to Agamemnon. Partiality, preference, after the decision or rather non-decision of the court, there needs must be. And her preference will be not for the woman.

Now doubtless it is not in this way that an English Aeschylus might be expected to deal with the practical question of the release. We should expect rather an encomium upon mercy, or a reliance upon our popular principle (so-called) that innocence is to be assumed until guilt is established. And we might find, in commentaries on the *Eumenides*, phrases which point in this direction; we might find hints of it, praises of φιλανθρωπία, and the φιλανθρωπία of Athena in particular, in Greek oratory. But in the *Eumenides* we shall not find them, either here or anywhere. Nowhere is there the least suggestion that the release of the defendant follows naturally, presumptively, and in preference to punishment, upon the equal division of the tribunal.

The position thus taken is remarkable; but is it

not logical? Does it not show in the Athenian poet, and in the Athenian mind generally, if Aeschylus here follows a tradition, a certain boldness and clearness in facing fundamental problems? The principle of a popular judicature, that is to say, of decision by average opinion, to which the Athenians, like ourselves, attached great importance, does really· involve, if pushed home, the admission that, in cases of great moral difficulty, no determination, deserving to be distinguished as just, can be had. For opinion may in reality be equally divided, in which case the instrument fails. The Areopagus in such cases dismissed the defendant, but was content to base this practice merely on an imaginary precedent: Athena, the patron-goddess, had voted for a particular defendant in an ancient and famous trial. The practice, that is to say, was a practice, and nothing more was pretended. Aeschylus, exhibiting this very trial, is compelled to quit the ground of precedent, but adheres to logic in carefully separating the practical question from the judicial, and tracing the practical decision to external circumstances, personal, casual, and manifestly not constituting a ground in reason either for the act or for the subsequent imitation of it.

It is thus that we should understand the emphatic words with which the goddess prefaces her vote, ἐμὸν τόδ' ἔργον, 'Here is a task *for me.*' Naturally (I do not say necessarily but naturally) this reminds us by contrast of her equally emphatic protest against taking a judicial part in the trial: 'If it be thought by some that this matter is too great for mortal man to judge— yet neither is it fit for me to discriminate passionate pleas in a cause of blood[1].' The suggestion is, that, in such a contest as that of Orestes, even to give sentence requires a sympathy with passion not properly attributable to the serene and intellectual patroness of Athens. Wide as is the gulf which separates our own religious and imaginative symbols from those of Aeschylus, it is not, I think, difficult to understand here his lofty and impressive turn of thought. We suppose then naturally that the decision, which Athena describes as 'a task for her', is something different in kind from that which she has repudiated, and not open to the like objection. And such a difference there is, if what she undertakes to decide is a practical matter, totally independent of the pleas and the question of right. No passion, nor sympathy with passion, is involved in what is given expressly as a mere fancy, a personal and casual preference. So also we account for her brevity and what in Aeschylus we must call the lightness of her tone, contrasting strongly with the force of Apollo and the solemnity of the Erinyes, nay, with the majesty of Athena herself, in the speech with which she proclaims the foundation of the court, and in other places. It is hard to suppose that a plea so magnificently conducted is determined judicially, according to the conception of Aeschylus, by three verses, which add not a jot to the argument. So also, and hardly, I think, otherwise, we may find intelligible and sincere the position taken by Athena when endeavouring to pacify the Furies after the dismissal of the cause: that, the votes on the cause being equal, they have sustained no defeat[2]. With what grace, or

---

[1] *vv.* 470 foll.　　　　[2] *v.* 795, etc.

what sense, can Athena say this, if, but for the vote of Athena, the prosecutors actually obtained a majority in a tribunal established by herself? Here also she assumes that her ruling, though called a vote, is not properly speaking a vote in the cause, a vote upon the pleas. The plea of right, by the equal division of the best available and only appropriate tribunal, a human jury, has been left undetermined ; and the sequel, an accident of place and person, imports ' no defeat in the cause' to either side. The distinction is subtle, but it is not unintelligible ; and without it, the consolation offered by Athena must, I think, appear frivolous and insulting.

I have noticed before, that the question we are discussing could not arise, if we could determine certainly the number, odd or even, of the Areopagite jurors in the play. Personally I believe that the number was *ten*, or some multiple of ten, and take this to be the most natural, though not inevitable, interpretation of the *ten* couplets, five from the prosecutors and five from the defending advocate (Apollo), which accompany and punctuate the voting[1]. From the little that is known respecting the history of the Areopagus may be drawn considerations either in favour of a jury numbering ten (or tens), or against it. The point would be almost determined, and in favour of ten, if we might see a reference to this number in the declaration of Athena, at the beginning of her foundation-speech[2], that ' this place (the hill of Areopagus) shall henceforth be the place of council for δεκαστοί'—αἰεὶ δεκαστῶν τοῦτο βουλευτήριον. Tradition gives these very letters, δεκαστων, but divides them, unintelligibly

---

[1] *vv.* 711—730. 　　　　　　[2] *v.* 683.

and wrongly as all agree, into the two words δὲ ἑκάστων. The word δεκάζειν, 'to count or make up a ten or tens,' seems to have been used originally at Athens, as the exactly equivalent *decuriare* at Rome, for the process of selecting and, as we say, empanelling a jury. Both words, being employed euphemistically for the process of packing or bribing a jury, fell eventually into disrepute. But I do not myself think it impossible that Aeschylus used δεκαστός, 'made up by ten or tens', in the proper and higher signification, and that αἰεὶ δεκαστῶν, 'those empanelled from time to time', should be so read and interpreted. This, if true, would greatly strengthen the reasons for thinking that the Areopagites exhibited in the play are δεκαστοί, ten or tens in number. It would be also characteristic of Aeschylus to find a mystical significance in the number, as he does for the *seventh* gate in the *Seven Against Thebes*. For this he might plead authority[1];

---

[1] Schol. to Aristotle *Metaphysics*, I. 5 (p. 985 *b* 26); see Berlin ed. Vol. IV. p. 541 *b*: Pythagorean doctrines respecting the symbolical signification of numbers, and particularly of the symbolical number for *justice*. After quoting and explaining views in favour of *four*, *nine*, and *five* (the last of which turns upon the relation of that number to the *decad*) the commentator adds: ἔνιοι δέ φασιν ὅτι ὡς μεταξὺ τῆς δεκάδος ὢν ὁ ε΄ δικαστὴς ἐκαλεῖτο τοῖς Πυθαγορείοις, οἷόν τις διχαστὴς ὤν. Now this mystical connexion of δικάζειν (*judge*) and διχάζειν (*divide*) is apparently adduced by Aeschylus himself as a point in favour of *judging by division*, that is to say by the votes of a jury, when Athena says (*Eum.* 487) κρίνασα δ᾽ ἀστῶν τῶν ἐμῶν τὰ βέλτατα | ἥξω, διαιρεῖν τοῦτο πρᾶγμ᾽ ἐτητύμως. Here ἐτητύμως, according to the general use of this word by Aeschylus, suggests an etymological point (see my edition of the *Seven Against Thebes*, *Appendix*), which is found in the double bearing of διαιρεῖν (δικάζειν-διχάζειν). All this would lead up excellently to a court of *ten* (or *tens*) and the equal division of such a court upon a case truly equal and insoluble. The mystical connexion is thus extended to δεκάζειν-δικάζειν-διχάζειν.— The 'obvious' conjecture δικαστῶν (Canter) for δ᾽ ἑκάστων in *Eum.* 684 appears to me, from a critical point of view, not entertainable.

and there are indications of such a purpose in the
Eumenides itself. And of course *ten*, or any even
number of Areopagites, would decisively prove that
the additional vote of Athena does not make equality.
I note this in passing, because, though the legal sense
of δεκάζειν has been brought into connexion with this
enigmatical αἰεὶ δ᾽ ἑκάστων, the precise view which I
suggest, has not, so far as I know, been considered.

Again, the ambiguity of Athena's words might be
cleared, if we could supply her action, if we had
authoritative stage-directions. 'This my vote I shall
add to Orestes,' or 'I shall reckon as added'—προσθήσομαι. The word seems compatible with either of
these renderings. Which is meant, and what did the
actor do? Shall we suppose that, after the brief
exposition of her motive, the goddess, proceeding, as
the jurors have done, to the urns, actually puts in her
pebble, and then, but not till then, having returned to
her place, makes the statement that equality absolves
the defendant? This action is admissible; and it would
go far to prove that the ballots, which she next com-
mands to be taken from the urns, and which are
presently declared to be equally divided, include the
one which she herself has put in. But it is also sup-
posable that she does not quit her place, nor actually
put in a pebble, but signifies merely by gesture, by
raised hand and extended arm, her will that a vote for
her shall be 'reckoned' upon the side of discharge.
It may be thought that such action, such a difference
between her and the human jurors, is more consistent
with her dignity, and better in scenic effect. And we
have in Euripides, as I have formerly taken occasion
to remark, a description of this voting, which *may* be

explained as referring to such a gesture. ' The equality of votes,' says the Orestes of the *Iphigenia in Taurica*, 'was differentiated in my favour by Pallas *with her arm*[1].' This ὠλένη, *with her arm*, is enigmatical. Many pronounce it nonsense, and they may be right, but that is not certain. If Athena voted by gesture, by the extended arm, and if this attitude, either as devised by Aeschylus or given by tradition, was celebrated (as we may well suppose), the allusion of Euripides would be explicable. At all events such action is quite compatible with the Aeschylean text, and will be almost decisive (if we assume it) for the view that no pebble of Athena is included among those which are taken from the urns and found equal.

One other detail we may notice, in the language and wording of our passage, which I have deferred to this place because, among all arguments drawn from the passage itself, I think it perhaps the weightiest. If the motive alleged by Athena, her peculiar parentage, is not the ground of her ruling upon the possible case of an equal division, if the motive belongs to a vote, distinct from the ruling,—then the ruling itself has no declared motive at all. Now I am far from saying that such a treatment would be bad in principle. Whatever we may choose to say, in a confused and popular way of thinking, no true reason, no argument founded on the nature of right, can be given for not punishing, any more than for punishing, an act of which the moral quality remains, after the fullest and

---

[1] Eur. *Iph. T.* 965 :   ἴσας δέ μοι
ψήφους διηρίθμιζε Παλλὰς ὠλένῃ.
v.l. διηρίθμησε. See *Euripides the Rationalist*, p. 188.

best consideration, indeterminate. Nor does Aeschylus pretend any true reason ; and if the arbitrary action of his Athena were taken without any motive expressed, nothing could be objected in logic. But for drama, for the movement of the scene, some pretext, however casual and irrelevant, seems to be, not necessary perhaps, but certainly desirable.

But in truth it is not upon the details of our passage that the interpretation of it should be rested. Of these, on both sides of the dispute, enough has been said, and hardly enough, I think, about the relation of the Areopagitic trial to the scheme of the play and the problems of the entire trilogy. The tremendous discords of the *Agamemnon* and the *Choephori* are not to be solved—and the harmony of the *Eumenides* assumes that in some way they are soluble—by methods of political compromise or legal procedure ; and if Aeschylus pretended that they are, his facility in laying the spectre would strangely contrast with his obstinacy in raising it. The difficulty, which thinking men must feel, in determining the degree and nature of moral responsibility, is not limited by local beliefs or temporary usages. Evil and crime seem to be actually produced, at least in part, by forces not clearly distinguishable, for us, from the power which condemns and punishes. There *is*, notwithstanding the shallow sarcasm of the cynic in Shakespeare, there *is*, or there seems to be, such a thing as the 'divine thrusting on.' And in the last resort, so Aeschylus declares in words which none who reads them ever forgets, we cannot throw off the burden of such reflexions otherwise than upon a something or someone—that we know not how

to name, Ζεύς, ὅστις ποτ᾽ ἐστίν[1]. The story of Agamemnon, the story of Orestes, as shaped and coloured
by Aeschylus, are but illustrations of a dilemma which
did not begin with the practice of consulting prophets
like Calchas, or oracles like that of Delphi, and most
certainly did not end with the institution of courts such
as the Areopagus.

The *Eumenides* is doubtless, in one aspect, an
encomium upon the Areopagus, and upon trial by
jury as an element in the evolution of Athens. No
such efficient guardian of society was to be found, we
are told, either southward in the Peloponnese, or
northward to the far side of Macedonia, οὔτ᾽ ἐν Σκύ-
θαισιν οὔτε Πέλοπος ἐν τόποις[2]. And we have reason
to think that this claim, if contemptibly moderate in
comparison with the world-wide prospects of modern
states, was true as far as it went. At the moment
when the *Orestea* was produced, the jurisdiction of the
Athenian courts seemed not unlikely to comprehend
before long an area then estimated as enormous; and if
Aeschylus and the Athenians held that mankind would
gain by this extension, their opinion was in no way
absurd. But in the scheme of the play, as related to
the trilogy, all these things are secondary. The trial
of Orestes, in the spiritual process towards the divine
harmony of the close, is but an indecisive incident,
and could be no more. Aeschylus is not so false
and vulgar, as to make an Athenian jury anticipate
the judgment of the Eternal; we are not to suppose
that the ineffable Name, which the elders of the
Agamemnon cannot find, proves at the last to be

[1] *Ag.* 160.   [2] *v.* 703.

simply Areopagus, or 'the Judicial Committee of the Privy Council.'

I do not for a moment suggest that any one does so suppose; but the danger of such misunderstanding seems to be too little considered, when we allow it for probable that the verdict or non-verdict of the jury includes, as one item, a judicial opinion from the goddess Athena.

The equal votes of the Areopagites settle nothing whatever; they merely reduce to numerical precision the lesson of the foregoing plays, that, in the world as it is, human judgment is often (and if often, why not always?) at a loss whether to absolve or condemn. To the desperate cry of the *Choephori* for a final peace,

$$\pi o\hat{\iota} \ \kappa\alpha\tau\alpha\lambda\acute{\eta}\xi\epsilon\iota$$
$$\mu\epsilon\tau\alpha\kappa o\iota\mu\iota\sigma\theta\grave{\epsilon}\nu \ \mu\acute{\epsilon}\nu os \ \ddot{\alpha}\tau\eta s;$$

the best tribunal in the world replies by a confession of nullity. It will neither condemn nor absolve.

And indeed, the judgment is taken in circumstances precluding even the hope of determining in this way the general and spiritual problems which underlie the particular case. These are determined, or rather it is assumed that in some mystic and superhuman manner they are determinable, when the Erinyes, for no reason whatever, but influenced, we know not how, by Athena, became patrons and defenders of that institution which, prospectively and retrospectively, they have denounced as a fraud upon justice. But to this reconciliation the sentence of the court, if such it can be called, contributes nothing; and no sentence, not even one against Orestes and, so far, in favour of the Erinyes, could have contributed. For the Erinyes, adding a new and terrible ἀπορία or problem to those accumulated in the foregoing story, object from the first, and upon grounds neither answered nor answerable, not to the judgment or the law, but to the tribunal and trial. Justice, according to them, is already denied and overthrown, when a sinner, amenable to them, has even the prospect and chance of acquittal :

νῦν καταστροφαὶ νέων
θεσμίων, εἰ κρατήσει δίκα τε καὶ βλάβα
τοῦδε μητροκτόνου [1].

Justice, as they conceive it, is essentially immutable, sin, where they recognize it, essentially unpardonable, both here and hereafter. If not, if guilt is always a question of circumstances and matter of opinion, πίτνει δόμος δίκας [2], the House of Justice comes to the ground. Right is a word without any real foundation.

Upon this point the Furies are adamantine. By every device of poetry and art their implacable, undeviating, interminable pursuit is realised and enforced ; and the perfectly true proposition, that the mere existence of such a thing as a criminal tribunal is, from one point of view, a denial of justice, is driven in upon the least willing mind. Under this light, the problem, what should justly be done with Orestes, becomes scarcely visible in the embracing theorem, that, so far as we actually see, no justice does certainly exist. And in fact, after the dismissal of the defendant, his personal case, not being in truth the matter of controversy between the superhuman disputants, is never mentioned again. Their controversy exists before the

[1] *Eum.* 307 foll., 490 foll. and the play *passim.*   [2] *Eum.* 516.

trial, survives the trial, must necessarily survive it, and by nothing, which occurs in the trial, could possibly be affected.

Now with these, the general lines of the play and trilogy, we surely require, for consistency, that the equal division of the Areopagus shall be truly and absolutely equal, equal in weight as well as in number ; and also, that the judgment of the tribunal shall be an ordinary human judgment, having indeed as good a claim to represent eternal right and the eternal mind as any judgment here procurable can have, but not a better or a transcendent claim. But how can it be so regarded, if one of the so-called units in the balance is a judicial opinion on the merits proceeding from the Daughter of Zeus ? The difficulties of human justice, and all the distracting questions that the trilogy propounds and illustrates, arise precisely because no such judgment is here procurable. Judgment by peers supposes parity among the judges. How could we talk of equality or plurality in a jury composed of Areopagites (so many) and an Intelligence of Heaven, a jury of eleven men and an Archangel ? The judgment of Athena, if she gave any, must obliterate the rest, and should be, in itself, decisive. And indeed it must be considered, upon this view, a most fortunate thing that the human jurors did not give an actual majority, which they nearly did, against Orestes and against the opinion, subsequently expressed, of the goddess. Suppose they had, and that the votes (including, or not including, Athena's) had numbered (let us say) 50 in all, and had proved to be 24 for acquittal and 26 for condemnation. What then ? Are we to imagine that, in this case, Orestes would have been delivered by the goddess, as president, to the Furies, in obedience to one or even two unnamed Athenians, and in spite of her expressed opinion that, in justice, he ought to be acquitted? Surely such a conception would be profane and grotesque.

But no such paradox, and no such inconsistency with the general lines of the work, is required by the supposition that, judgment failing, Athena decides, upon a casual preference, irrelevant to the merits, what is to be done. Upon this view, both the division of the court and the practical ruling of the goddess leave the question of right precisely where it was, the division because it is equal and null, the ruling because it is not a judgment. The lesson of the trial is this, that a well-chosen jury is indeed the best judicial instrument available to man, a boon so great that religious feeling would naturally assign it to a superhuman origin, and suppose for it a divine sanction; but on the other hand, the fact that we have no better judicial instrument, that in the last analysis what we call 'justice' is never anything more than a balance of opinion, is a signal illustration of our weakness, our inability to reach the eternal foundation of things. For in cases of difficulty, in test-cases, the balance of opinion should be supposed equal, and then, though we do and must act, we act at hazard, upon a rule (if we have a rule for the case) which cannot have any reason at all, and which, if we are honest, we shall admit (as the Athenians did admit it) to be arbitrary.

We expect the judgment of Zeus, 'the perfect witness of all-judging Jove'; but here we have it not.

And if we will suppose, as it seems (or seemed to Aeschylus) intolerable not to suppose, that in some way the groping, ineffectual processes of this world are justifiable, that is an act of faith, which transcends argument and, if exhibited in symbol, must be exhibited as a mystery. We may say, if we will, that the Erinyes—'Furies' is a bad translation, for Aeschylean purposes very bad, and one would gladly be rid of it — that the Erinyes, the representatives of unfailing punishment, could be induced to bless, and do bless, our tribunals, though these are the very embodiment of uncertainty and mutability ; but we must not say that this blessing is extorted or procured by the logical merit of our sentences and executions. It is not by the vote of the citizens that Athena, in the end, obtains the concurrence of her divine opponents ; and still less is it by her arbitrary disposal of the defendant. After all this, the Erinyes are implacable as ever. And not until Aeschylus has made this point perfectly clear, does he exhibit that sudden and miraculous conversion, that satisfactory but altogether mysterious and unexplained reconciliation, which proclaims that, beyond these voices, there is an eternal peace[1].

But the intrusion into the trial of a judicial vote on the part of Athena, or even a declaration of her mind upon the guilt or innocence of Orestes, would, as it seems to me, upset altogether the scheme of Aeschylus' thought and the significance of his picture. The

[1] On the conversion of the Eumenides, I would refer to a lecture delivered to the *Classical Association of England and Wales* at their meeting in January 1906, and to be published in their *Proceedings*.

unabated hostility of the Furies becomes, upon this reading, the mere wilfulness or brutality of inferior creatures. Their subsequent appeasement contributes nothing of value to the conclusion; and we should wonder why Aeschylus has invested them with so much dignity, or why he abandoned what appears to have been the true and original version of the legend, that after the trial the defeated fiends fled in impotent disgust to their nether darkness. This version is mentioned by Euripides in the epilogue to his *Electra*, where he seems to be merely citing mythological traditions and has certainly no motive for innovation. It is far more simple, and more agreeable to the processes of unreflective minds, than the mystical reconcilement pictured, and in all probability invented, by Aeschylus. Euripides, to whose interests and convictions the whole myth was indifferent, no part of religion at all, is content, for theatrical purposes, to give the tradition in its native crudity. For the author of the *Prometheus*, mythology had another value; he alters in order to preserve.

In this brief sketch, I of course make no pretence even to summarize all that can be brought to bear, more or less immediately, upon our theme. I have said nothing about the much debated question, what number or numbers, if any, were established or admitted in the composition of an Areopagitic jury, nor of the question, strangely little considered, by whom or how such a jury was actually selected. I cannot discuss the scribble upon our MS. of the *Eumenides*, which states that 'the Areopagites', whatever that means, were 31. Those who do discuss it, commonly begin with the disquieting supposition that the writer meant 51, whereby we bring him into touch with our perplexing and dubious fragments of information about the Ephetae, the legislation of Draco, and so forth. Nor can I consider the much more pertinent legend, which makes the jury, in the case of Orestes, to be the Twelve Gods, 12 therefore in number.

It is, I think, easy to overestimate the weight of such external considerations in the interpretation of a work of art. Compared with considerations drawn from the play itself, and founded upon what we *know* to have been present to the mind of the playwright, external matter is insignificant. We cannot be sure that either playwright or audience would have attached any importance to it. Without any disrespect to Aeschylus and the Athenians, it may well be doubted whether he or his contemporaries generally knew much about the archaeology of the Areopagus, the Ephetae, and the legislation of Draco, or had any such fixed conception of the first criminal trial as would prevent an artist from shaping the procedure in whatever way was best suited to exhibit his own idea. The student of history has views very different from those of the average contemporary, and knows much which, as a critic of art, he will do well to forget, because an artist, not working for students, was at liberty to ignore it. Even historical plays make, for the most part, very little pretence to satisfy the historian ; and for Aeschylus the historical element was almost negligible. The historical conscience, and the legal knowledge, of his audience cannot have had sufficient consistency to inspire respect, or to embarrass him in his proper function, the spectacular exhibition of his idea.

The general colour of the play does not suggest that the poet concerned himself much with erudition of any kind, historical or legal. Nothing is more striking than the absence from the play of those local touches, which he could have given in abundance. The specific features of the place of judgment, the Areopagus Hill, are ignored almost entirely. The Acropolis is pictured (if it is pictured at all) in a fashion so slight and symbolical, that we actually dispute, and cannot determine, whether or not the Acropolis, as distinct from the Areopagus, furnishes the playwright with a scene. Mythological traditions (so far as we know them) are set aside without scruple, if they do not suit the Aeschylean idea.

The idea, to artist and audience, is everything. By that, by the frame of the whole, we should be guided in the provisional preference of an interpretation, where the words of the document appear to leave ambiguity. Now the idea of the *Eumenides* seems to be this. A discord, a fundamental contradiction, appears between two qualities, both of which we would fain attribute to justice—fixity and equity. Hence the uncertainty of our moral judgments, an uncertainty, which, it is easy to see, is the very cause and matter of tragedy. To each side of the dilemma Aeschylus assigns superhuman representatives, who disagree, each with irrefragable reason, on the question whether human justice, justice as administered among men, can be truly just. When, by a test-case, tried according to the best method

practicable, the divine dispute has been shown to
admit of no human conciliation, we are consoled and
fortified by a *mystical* reconcilement, commended to
our acceptance by the beauty with which it is invested.
The assurance, which reason cannot give, is reached by
an appeal to faith.   The Avengers (we know not why)
approve in retrospect an act of mercy ; and the validity
of law, in the best form known among men, is certified
by a picture of divine peace, which we accept as true,
not upon any argument, but moved by our moral
desire, not because we *can* discover justice, but because
we *will*.

The mystical reconciliation is attributed by Athena
to Zeus, whose name (we saw) is recognized by
Aeschylus in the *Agamemnon* as the best available
symbol, though not adequate, for the object of his
faith, the solver of human doubts.   The same reserve,
the same jealous determination to accept no final term
for an infinite mystery, is shown in the last words of
the *Eumenides*, when the achieved concord is rested
not even upon 'Zeus', but upon a 'condescension' or
compact between the personal 'Zeus' and the almost
impersonal symbol of 'Moira' or Destiny.   Throughout
the play, the name of 'Moira', and the still vaguer
plural 'Moirai', is associated with the more ancient
dynasty, of which Zeus is not only heir but also
adversary, and which the Erinyes, the Avengeresses,
themselves represent and champion.   The rehabilita-
tion of justice, the repair of the sceptical ruin in
which 'the House of Justice' is left by the ambiguous
result of the trial, is to the last presented as the work
of some influence, power, spell, operation, which tran-

scends the faculties of human thought and language, a fusion of opposites, not to be covered by any single name, nor by any such one-sided conception as that of 'victory'. All this is thoroughly consistent with the poet's mind as exhibited in the *Prometheus* and elsewhere; it is the attitude of a mystic.

We should not easily believe, that this author was guilty of an oversight and error so inconsistent with his apparent purpose, as to put into one scale of his earthly tribunal a judgment from the Daughter of Zeus, and to propound, in words of his own, reasons upon which that judgment is founded. The equipoise, the ambiguity, which creates the opportunity and necessity for the solution by faith, is thus destroyed; we are assumed to know, and to be capable of proving, that the earthly tribunal does administer justice, to know this, and not merely to believe it; and the mystical coalition, by which the divine opponents of the tribunal agree to bless it, becomes a superfluity, a symbol without interest or content. Aeschylus was no doubt capable of error, but he is entitled, like any one else, to a presumption in favour of his consistency, especially upon the main lines of his thought and composition. Where, as in our passage, his words, in themselves, leave a mere doubt, a perfectly indeterminate choice, the construction favourable to his consistency, though not demonstrable, seems to be something better than the better opinion.

On the whole therefore, while admitting both opinions of our passage as possible, and reserving a place for any real proof which may be discovered on either side, I do not think it necessary, or even just to the poet, to preserve, in the meantime, an absolutely open mind. In the absence of demonstration to the contrary, the proposition that the 'vote' of Athena in the *Eumenides* is not a judicial vote, not an opinion on the merits of the case, and therefore is not included in the equal division of the tribunal, should be regarded as an article of commentatorial faith.

WALTER HEADLAM

THE SECOND CHORUS OF THE
AGAMEMNON

THE SECOND CHORUS OF THE *AGAMEMNON*.

Clytemnestra has just finished her brilliant description of the beacons, by which, as she declares, Agamemnon has signalled to her across the sea the news of his success—the fall of Troy and the defeat of Priam and his son, the sinner Paris. This circumstantial account the Elders accept—at any rate for the moment—as convincing evidence, and thereupon break out into a *Te Deum* for the victory. They open with preliminary anapaests to the effect, 'This is the Lord's doing; it is Zeus of Hospitality that I acknowledge as the author of this act: if his vengeance has been long in coming, it has only been deferred in order that the blow might fall the surer.' Then the lyric takes up that declaration and pursues it.

"Διὸς πλαγὰν ἔχουσιν" εἰπεῖν   379
πάρεστιν, τοῦτό τ᾽ ἐξιχνεῦσαι·   380
ἔπραξεν ὡς ἔκρανεν. οὐκ ἔφα τις
θεοὺς βροτῶν ἀξιοῦσθαι μέλειν
ὅσοις ἀθίκτων χάρις
πατοῖθ᾽· ὃ δ᾽ οὐκ εὐσεβής·
πέφανται δ᾽ ἐκτίνουσ᾽   385
ἀτολμήτων ἀρὴ
πνεόντων μεῖζον ἢ δικαίως,
φλεόντων δωμάτων ὑπέρφευ,
ὑπὲρ τὸ βέλτιστον. ἔστω δ᾽ ἀπή-
μαντον ὥστ᾽ ἀπαρκεῖν
εὖ πραπίδων λαχόντα.
οὐ γὰρ ἔστιν ἔπαλξις
πλούτου πρὸς κόρον ἀνδρὶ
λακτίσαντι μέγαν Δίκας
βωμὸν εἰς ἀφάνειαν.   395

βιᾶται δ᾽ ἁ τάλαινα Πειθώ,
προβούλου παῖς ἄφερτος "Ατας·   397

379 ἔχουσαν altered to ἔχουσ᾽ Flor. ἔχουσιν Farn. 'De vera distinguendi
ratione nemo semel monitus dubitabit. Διὸς πλαγὰν ἔχουσι. *Jovis ictum habent.*'
Blomfield: but few have heeded. εἰπεῖν πάρεστιν is 'that judgment may be
pronounced indeed'; as in *Theb.* 906, and Philemon *frag.* 108 'καλὸν τὸ θνή-
σκειν᾽ ἔστιν ἐπὶ τούτῳ λέγειν.—With these words they take up the declaration of
v. 374.

380 τοῦτ᾽ ἐξιχνεῦσαι MSS.: τοῦτό τ᾽ Boissonade.

385 πέφανται δ᾽ **ἐκτίνουσ᾽** ἀτολμήτων **ἀρή**: the MS. reading is πέφανται δ᾽
                                                        κ
ἐγγόνουσ (**ἐγγόνουσ** Farn.) ἀτολμήτων **ἄρη** πνεόντων μεῖζον ἢ δικαίωσ, which is
meaningless. We can quickly clear the ground; for a little reflection will admit
what Karsten and Weil have pointed out, that there is no place here either for
ἐκγόνους or for "Αρη πνεόντων: Paris, who is the sinner (*v.* 409), has paid for his
sin in his own person; and the subject of the passage is the retribution ·following
sin that comes through a spirit made insolent with riches; whereas "Αρη πνεόντων
μεῖζον᾽ ἢ δικαίως would condemn him for a spirit *over-bellicose!* Hartung's reading
therefore, ἐκτίνουσ|α τόλμα τῶν "Αρη πνεόντων κτέ., besides giving an unparalleled

I 1

"*Struck by the hand of Zeus!*" ay, truth indeed,
And traceable : 'tis the act of will decreed
And purpose.   Under foot when mortals tread
Fair lovely Sanctities, the Gods, one said,
The easy Gods are careless :—'twas profane !
Here are sin's wages manifest and plain,
The sword's work on that swelled presumptuousness,
With affluent mansions teeming in excess,
Beyond Best Measure :—best, and sorrow-free,
The wise well-dowered mind's unharmed Sufficiency !

The Rich man hath no tower,
Whose Pride, in Surfeit's hour,
Kicks against high-enthroned Right
And spurns her from his sight.

I 2

Child of designing Ate's deadly womb,
The wretch Temptation drives him to his doom.

caesura, is untenable for sense : nevertheless the chief part of the credit is due to him for **ἐκτίνουσα**.   For ἄρη I merely restore **ἀρή**, *havoc, destruction by the sword*, a word used by Aeschylus in *Supp.* 86.   No accusative is now required with ἐκτίνουσα, because ἀρή is itself the penalty—a turn of phrase exactly paralleled in *v.* 1512 Ἄρης δίκας πάχνᾳ κουροβόρῳ παρέξει.   There is the same conception in 760—6 (δαίμονα τίταν) and in *Cho.* 643 (τίνειν μύσος).

The best illustration of the whole passage is a chorus very closely imitating it in Eur. *H.F.*, for which see *Class. Rev.* 1901, p. 104.   This should be studied attentively from *v.* 747 ἀντίποινα δ' ἐκτίνων τόλμα to the end ἃ νῦν ἐσορῶντι φαίνει ξιφηφόρων ἐς ἀγώνων ἅμιλλαν εἰ τὸ δίκαιον θεοῖς ἔτ' ἀρέσκει.

395 **εἰς ἀφάνειαν**: that is ὅταν τὴν δίκην τις ἀφανίσῃ.   Trag. frag. in Stob. Ecl. I. 3. 45 ἄφρονες δ' ὁπόσοι τὸ δίκαιον ἄγουσ' ὑπὸ τᾶς ἀδίκου βιοτᾶς ἀφανές.

397 **προβουλόπαις ἄφερτος Ἄτας** of the MS. is not a metrical line at all, apart from strophic correspondence.   **προβούλου παῖς** (Hartung) is right : Soph. *frag.* 533 ποικιλομήτιδες ἆται, *Cho.* 645 τέκνον δ' ἐπεισφέρει δόμοις αἱμάτων παλαιτέρων τίνειν μύσος χρόνῳ κλυτὰ βυσσόφρων 'Ερινύς, like Hecate in *Macbeth*, 'the close contriver of all harms.'   πρόβουλοσ παῖσ was probably the first stage in the error.

ἄκος δὲ παμμάταιον· οὐκ ἐκρύφθη,
πρέπει δέ, φῶς αἰνολαμπές, σίνος·
κακοῦ δὲ χαλκοῦ τρόπον
τρίβῳ τε καὶ προσβολαῖς
μελαμπαγὴς πέλει
δικαιωθείς (ἐπεὶ
διώκει παῖς ποτανὸν ὄρνιν),
πόλει πρόστριμμα θεὶς ἄφερτον·   405
λιτᾶν δ' ἀκούει μὲν οὔτις θεῶν·
τὸν δ' ἐπίστροφον τῶν
φῶτ' ἄδικον καθαιρεῖ.
οἷος καὶ Πάρις ἐλθὼν
ἐς δόμον τὸν Ἀτρειδᾶν
ᾔσχυνε ξενίαν τράπε-
ζαν κλοπαῖσι γυναικός.

λιποῦσα δ' ἀστοῖσιν ἀσπίστορας
κλόνους λογχίμους τε καὶ ναυβάτας ὁπλισμούς,
ἄγουσά τ' ἀντίφερνον Ἰλίῳ φθοράν,
βέβακεν ῥίμφα διὰ πυλᾶν,
ἄτλητα τλᾶσα· πολλὰ δ' ἔστενον
τάδ' ἐννέποντες δόμων προφῆται·   418
" ἰὼ ἰὼ δῶμα δῶμα καὶ πρόμοι,
ἰὼ λέχος καὶ στίβοι φιλάνορες.
πάρεστι σιγὰς ἀτίμους ἀλοιδόρους   421
. . . . ἀφημένων ἰδεῖν·
πόθῳ δ' ὑπερποντίας
φάσμα δόξει δόμων ἀνάσσειν.

---

405 Wilamowitz-Moellendorff restored the words to their proper order: what the MS. gives, πόλει πρόστριμμ' ἄφερτον θείς, is merely a case of *simplex ordo*, as explained in my paper on Transposition of Words *Class. Rev.* 1902, p. 243.

418 δόμων προφῆται 'spokesmen of the house' are members of Menelaus' household whose gossip voiced abroad the condition of affairs within. These revelations they convey in guarded language like the Chorus in the *Choephoroe* 45—82, not mentioning names, but saying πρόμοι, ἀφημένων, ὑπερποντίας, ἀνδρί, τις.

Then cure is all in vain. The vice he wears
He cannot hide ; sinister gleam declares
His mischief ; as base metal at the touch
And trial of the stone, he showeth smutch
(This fond man like a child a-chase of wings),
And the awful taint on all his people brings :
To prayers is not an ear in Heaven ; one frown
All conversant with such calls guilty and pulls down.

Such Paris was, that ate
Within the Atridae's gate,
And then disgraced the Stranger's bread
By theft of woman wed.

II 1

To Argos hurrying tumult, thronging power
Of men-at-arms and men-at-oars bequeathing,—
To Ilium bringing death for her sole dower,—
Ah, tripping it through her gate she's flown,
A crime done !—Then did voices moan,
The secrets of the house in sorrow breathing :

" *The Home, woe, woe, the Home ! The Princes, woe !*
The impress where the wedded limbs yet show !
There yonder abject sits, where all may see,
Shamed, unreviling, silent, bowed indignity :
Pined so with his beyond-sea dream
Afar, so lovesick, he shall seem
The pale faint ghost of proud authority.

421 πάρεστι σιγᾶς ἄτιμος ἀλοίδορος ἄδιστος ἀφεμένων ἰδεῖν MSS., neither
sense nor metre : with σιγᾶς ἀτίμους ἀλοιδόρους Hermann restored both. The
corruption was introduced by some scribe who failed to perceive the construction
of πάρεστιν ἰδεῖν—thought that it required a nominative. Just the same thing
happened in Eur. *Tro.* 36 τὴν δ' ἀθλίαν τήνδ' εἴ τις εἰσορᾶν θέλει, πάρεστιν,
Ἑκάβην κειμένην πυλῶν πάρος : where inferior MSS. give πάρεστιν Ἑκάβη
κειμένη.

What ἄδιστος should be is uncertain.—ἀφημένων Dindorf, 'sitting apart';
used by Homer of Achilles sulking in his tent. Greek, like other Oriental
mourners, *sat* or grovelled on the ground ; ' By the waters of Babylon we sat
down and wept, remembering Zion.'

εὐμόρφων δὲ κολοσσῶν
ἔχθεται χάρις ἀνδρί,
ὀμμάτων δ' ἐν ἀχηνίαις
ἔρρει πᾶσ' Ἀφροδίτα.   427

ὀνειρόφαντοι δὲ πειθήμονες   429
πάρεισι δόξαι φέρουσαι χάριν ματαίαν·
μάταν γὰρ, εὖτ' ἂν ἐσθλά τις δοκῶν ὁρᾶν—   431
παραλλάξασα διὰ χερῶν
βέβακεν ὄψις οὐ μεθύστερον
πτεροῖς ὀπαδοῖς ὕπνου κελεύθων."   434
τὰ μὲν κατ' οἴκους ἐφ' ἑστίας ἄχη
τάδ' ἐστὶ καὶ τῶνδ' ὑπερβατώτερα·
τὸ πᾶν δ' ἀφ' Ἑλλανος αἴας συνορμένοις   437
πένθει' ἀτλησικάρδιος   438
δόμων ἑκάστου πρέπει·
πολλὰ γοῦν θιγγάνει πρὸς ἦπαρ·

427 **ὀμμάτων δ' ἐν ἀχηνίαις ἔρρει πᾶσ' Ἀφροδίτα** is precisely like an Orphic line quoted by Lobeck *Aglaophamus* p. 951, χειρῶν δ' ὀλλυμένων ἔρρεν πολυεργὸς Ἀθήνη 'with the destruction of hands, Athena (the goddess of handicraft) was clean gone': and so all spirit of love, love-sense, is departed in the lack of eyes, which are the channels of desire (ἵμερος), and were created, according to Empedocles, by Aphrodite.

429 **πενθήμονες** of the MSS. is contrary to the sense: **πειθήμονες** Housman ('si dicerentur πειθήμονες, intelligerem' Karsten) rightly: *v.* 286 ὀνείρων φάσματ' εὐπιθῆ.

431 This line has caused much trouble because the sentence has no finite verb; yet δοκῶν ὁρᾷ, the most plausible of the conjectures, cannot be right, because Greek never said δοκῶν ὁρῶ, always δοκῶ ὁρᾶν. The verb is in fact *omitted*, with dramatic effect: 'For oft as, dreaming that he beholds his joy, (*he would embrace*).' I have given many similar examples in *Class. Rev.* 1898, p. 246.

434 **κελεύθοις** MSS., an easy error for **κελεύθων** (Karsten): when there was the choice, Aeschylus can hardly have preferred to make the sense less lucid by an assonance less pleasant to the ear.

437 **τὸ πᾶν δ' ἀφ' ἑλλάδος αἴας** of the MSS. is impossible rhythm here: it would be a single unrepeated *logaoedic* figure in a stanza of quite different rhythm. Ἑλλανος Bamberger.

438 **πένθεια τλησικάρδιος** MSS.: I correct the adjective, giving it precisely the opposite sense. *P.V.* 169 τίς ὧδε τλησικάρδιος θεῶν ὅτῳ τάδ' ἐπιχαρῆ; τίς οὐ συνασχαλᾷ κακοῖς τεοῖσι; means 'Who is so *hard-hearted* as to exult? Who

Fair shapely marbles white
Vex the distasting sight,—
Lost in the lack of eyes that shone,
The warm love dead and gone.

II 2

" *Dream-shown, in flattering shape, come phantasies,*
With joy—nay, fond illusion all their bringing!
Blissful in vision there when heaven is his—
Ah, vanishing through his arms away
'Tis gone, with never pause or stay,
Fast on the fickle paths where Sleep is winging."

These are the one forlorn home's miseries,
And more exceeding bitter yet than these.
And what at large for all that host of war
Far hence, the general legion sped from Hellas shore?
Theirs in their several houses due
Is mourning and heart-broken rue—
Cause enough, sure, keen-touching to the core!

is there that does not feel grief and indignation?' But applied to *mourning*,
τλησικάρδιος would be a contradiction in terms: Hom. I 3 πένθεϊ δ' ἀτλήτῳ
βεβολήατο (Τ 367 ἄτλητον ἄχος, Apoll. Rhod. II. 858 κῆδος). Τ 18 τέτλαθι δή,
κραδίη· καὶ κύντερον ἄλλο ποτ' ἔτλης. Ε 382 τέτλαθι...καὶ ἀνάσχεο κηδομένη περ.
Ω 48 ἀλλ' ἦ τοι κλαύσας καὶ ὀδυράμενος μεθέηκεν· τλητὸν γὰρ μοῖραι θυμὸν θέσαν
ἀνθρώποισι. Archilochus 9. 5—10 ending τλῆτε, γυναικεῖον πένθος ἀπω-
σάμενοι. *Agam.* 886 τλᾶσ' ἀπενθήτῳ φρενί. *Anth. Pal.* VII. 335 τλῆθι
πένθος, εὔνασον δάκρυ. Hesychius who records τλασίφρονα: ὑπομονητικόν
'patient,' 'long-suffering,' 'stout-hearted,' records also the negative ἀτλησίφρων:
οὐδεμιᾶς τόλμης ἔννοιαν ἔχων: and, like this, '*broken-hearted*' is **ἀτλησικάρδιος.**

The critics have not seen that the dative **συνορμένοις** depends upon **πρέπει:**
what is proper for a victor is acclamation, as in Pind. *N*. 3. 67 βοᾷ δὲ νικαφόρῳ
σὺν 'Αριστοκλείδᾳ πρέπει: what is proper for the dead is regretful lamentation.
It is to πρέπει in that sense that **γοῦν** refers; there is reason in plenty why their
houses should behave so; well they may!

οὓς μὲν γάρ τις ἔπεμψεν
οἶδεν, ἀντὶ δὲ φωτῶν
τεύχη καὶ σποδὸς εἰς ἑκά-
στου δόμους ἀφικνεῖται.

ὁ χρυσαμοιβὸς δ᾽ Ἄρης σωμάτων   445
καὶ ταλαντοῦχος ἐν μάχῃ δορὸς
πυρωθὲν ἐξ Ἰλίου
φίλοισι πέμπει βαρὺ
ψῆγμα δυσδάκρυτον ἀν-
τήνορος σποδοῦ γεμί-
ζων λέβητας εὐθέτους.

στένουσι δ᾽ εὖ λέγοντες ἄνδρα τὸν μὲν ὡς μάχης ἴδρις,
τὸν δ᾽ ἐν φοναῖς καλῶς πεσόντ᾽—
" ἀλλοτρίας διαὶ γυναικός,"
τάδε σῖγά τις βαΰζει,
φθονερὸν δ᾽ ὑπ᾽ ἄλγος ἕρπει
προδίκοις Ἀτρείδαις.

οἱ δ᾽ αὐτοῦ περὶ τεῖχος
θήκας Ἰλιάδος γᾶς
εὔμορφοι κατέχουσιν· ἐχ-
θρὰ δ᾽ ἔχοντας ἔκρυψεν.

βαρεῖα δ᾽ ἀστῶν φάτις σὺν κότῳ·
δημοκράντου δ᾽ ἀρᾶς τίνει χρέος.
μένει δ᾽ ἀκοῦσαί τί μου
μέριμνα νυκτηρεφές·
τῶν πολυκτόνων γὰρ οὐκ
ἄσκοποι θεοί· κελαι-
ναὶ δ᾽ Ἐρινύες χρόνῳ   469
τυχηρὸν ὄντ᾽ ἄνευ δίκας

445 A fine example to show Aeschylus' power of developing an image and
sustaining it : the God of War is like a money-changer who gives gold for bulkier
metal ; but his dealing is in flesh and blood ; he has his scales like the money-
changer, but they are the scales of battle ; he receives a human body, a man's
bulk, and what he gives back in exchange is like the merchant's gold-dust
(ψῆγμα), *fined in the fire*, and *heavy*, for it causes heaviness ; and packed in
vessels which are **εὔθετοι**, a word covering two senses—'handy' *habiles*, and

From each home once there went
A man forth : him it sent
Each knows ; but what are these return ?
A little dust, an urn.

III 1

Ares, the Changer—of the Body's coin,
With scales poised—where the spears in battle join,
Fined in the furnace home from Ilium sends
Dust, heavy dust and sore to weeping friends,—
A live man's worth of ash, full-measured load
In small jars' compass decently bestowed!

Then wail the sorrowing kinsmen, and belaud each man,
This for a perfect soldier, how that fell
Glorious amid the carnage, fighting well—
  "*For another's wife!*" the growl comes low,
  And sores against their Princes grow,
    This process that began.

    Others possess their tomb
    There, in their beauty's bloom—
    Troy's holders, in the land they hold
    Graved, beneath hated mould!

III 2

A people's talk is dangerous when it storms ;
The effect of public curse their wrath performs.
For something cloaked within the night my mind
Stands listening :—the divine eyes are not blind
To men of blood : the man of mere success,
Luck's thriver in defect of Righteousness,

decently disposed' *bene compositi* applied to a corpse: Bekk. *An.* 40. 23 εὐθετεῖν, νεκρόν : τὸ εὖ κοσμεῖν ἐν τάφοις νεκρόν.   The last point has been missed.

469 Another image, developed out of the word ἀμαυρόν : Hesiod had said that when a man is prosperous unrighteously, ῥεῖα δέ μιν μαυροῦσι θεοί, μινύθουσι δὲ οἶκον *Op.* 325, and 280 ὃς δέ κε...δίκην βλάψας νήκεστον ἀασθῇ, τοῦ δέ τ᾽ ἀμαυροτέρη γενεὴ μετόπισθε λέλειπται.   The meaning of παλιντυχεῖ **τριβᾷ** βίου (which has not been understood) is 'with *detrition* by reverse fortune' wasting him away again.

παλιντυχεῖ τριβᾷ βίου
τιθεῖσ᾽ ἀμαυρόν· ἐν δ᾽ ἀί-
στοις τελέθοντος οὔτις ἀλκά.
τὸ δ᾽ ὑπερκόπως κλύειν εὖ
βαρύ· βάλλεται γὰρ ὄσσοις
Διόθεν κάρανα.   476
  κρίνω δ᾽ ἄφθονον ὄλβον·
μήτ᾽ εἴην πτολιπόρθης,
μήτ᾽ οὖν αὐτὸς ἁλοὺς ὑπ᾽ ἄλ-
λῳ βίον κατίδοιμι.

476 **κεραυνός** MS.: **κάρανα** Tucker, just what is required; the *eyes* are the jealous eyes of Zeus.

Consider for a moment what has happened. We began, as you remember, with an exultant hymn for triumph over Troy; and we have ended in the profoundest gloom of apprehension for the conqueror. We passed,—almost insensibly, through the masterly skill of the transitions—first from the sin of Paris to the flight of Helen; thence to the private sorrows of the deserted husband; then, in a single phrase which carried us in a sweep across the sea and back, to the public suffering of Greece at large—the warriors who have lost their lives abroad, and the mourning of their kinsmen in their several homes; thence to the covert murmurs of resentment—disaffection spreading like a gangrene in the people's hearts towards Agamemnon; and the dangers threatening him both from God and man.

And in the following scene we find the same effect repeated. The Herald enters full of joy and thank-

Doomed by the dark Avengers, wanes again at last,
Dwindling, until he fades out where the dim
Lost shadows are; and there, no help for him.—
　And Fame, too loudly when she cries,
　Is dangerous also; flashing eyes
　　Of Zeus the proud height blast.

　　Mine be the happy state
　　That moves no jealous hate;
　　No conquest, neither let me see
　　My own captivity.

---

fulness and enthusiasm—it is just because of the
disaffection towards Agamemnon which there is so
much reason to anticipate that he is at such pains to
bespeak him a good welcome. He does all he can to
confine their attention to the bright side,—but in vain:
the Elders force him to disclose the disaster to the fleet
and the loss of Menelaus; our bright hopes are dashed,
and we are left once more in deep despondency.

This is the poet whom criticism even in the time
of Aristophanes had begun to disparage with the
epithet ἀξύστατος—*incompositus*, as Quintilian translates
it; whatever may be the precise significance of the
term, it implies at any rate some defectiveness in
construction, composition, or vital unity of thought.

It is a defect which is certainly not apparent in the
plays that we possess. On the contrary, the more we
study them, the more, I think, we shall discover in
them what is to my mind the highest of artistic
qualities—the power of construction, of designing a
composition from the beginning to the end and

controlling the relations and proportions of one part to another ; the power that corresponds to strategy as opposed to tactics ; or the statesman's power as opposed to the mere politician's, the power that in art is exhibited in the highest degree by Beethoven.

Somewhat a remote analogy that may seem, perhaps ; but it was not merely fanciful or ornamental ; I used it with a definite meaning. A play of Aeschylus does seem to me to resemble more than anything a movement of a modern symphony ; a trilogy is three successive movements ; with a *scherzo*, the Satyric play, to follow. And his way of work is very much like that of modern musicians using themes and motives. He will have moral ideas and large figurative conceptions, lyrical in character, running through a whole play, which do not mar the vividness of the dramatic action, but like musical motives knit the whole frame up and give it just that σύστασις, or vital unity, which it has been the tradition to regard his plays as lacking.

For example, in the *Seven against Thebes* from the first phrase to the last and recurring through the play we have the figure of the storm-tossed Ship of State. In the *Choephoroe* the main conception of this kind is a change from Darkness into Light ; '*the Night is departed*' is the burden of the last chorus : and again the usurping tyrants in the palace are, as it were, a foul pollution or disease, to be purged out, or cut out with the knife. Those notions again to the mind of Aeschylus could hardly fail to suggest the analogy of the Great Mysteries, in which those initiated and made perfect after purifying ceremonies passed from profound darkness suddenly into a great light : and, as I have lately pointed out, more than one passage, but notably the last chorus, is to be interpreted as an allusion to them.

In the *Agamemnon*, the quarrel between Greece and Troy is like a case-at-law—that is one of these figurative ideas, a minor one. But the main one is contained, as I believe, in the first two stanzas of the chorus I have just quoted. There is much in them, I suspect, which will have seemed obscure : but the reason it appears obscure is this,—that it is all *allusion* to doctrines which the poet presupposed his audience to know, but which to us are not familiar as they should be.

There was a body of ideas which the Greek race had adopted or evolved as conclusions reached by man's experience—the maxims of the Seven Sages are among the earliest and simplest. These were accepted as established truths, and were the bases for the ordering of life. This is different from our ways, and we are not accustomed to it, because we do not live by proverbs; but the East does still, and the Greeks did. They may have had the defects of the quality, but they had the most serious intellectual love of truth, and they clung to these conclusions as the proved results of human science.

These ideas, already known—familiar for the most part as the Ten Commandments—the poets are constantly alluding to and founding metaphors upon ; they are like *themes* on which a musician composes variations; not themselves to be regarded as mere casual embroidery, but as the frame or base on which the fabric of the whole is built. Suppose you listen, say, to a remote variation of Beethoven's on *God Save the King*, it is certain you will appreciate much better what the artist is doing if you happen to have heard the tune before and bear it in your mind. So what we have to do is to become familiar with the themes. Until we are familiar with them, and can use that currency, we shall never be able to read Aeschylus or Pindar, or Sophocles or Euripides, or Greek literature generally, with the right intelligence.

Let me run briefly through the ideas in the first stanza. The subject is the inevitable retribution for Excess, ὑπὲρ τὸ βέλτιστον: that is, beyond due Measure or the Mean ; μέτρον ἄριστον or τὸ μέσον βέλτιστον was the characteristic axiom of the Greeks ; their ideal was the Harmless Mean, a modest competence, because Too Much brought Harm : 'Give me neither poverty nor riches'; 'The blessing of the Lord, it maketh rich, and he addeth no sorrow with it.' There are scores of passages, besides allusions, where that view is definitely stated.

And what follows was a train of sequence equally well recognised:—πλοῦτος or τρυφή, they said, excessive wealth or luxury, leads to κόρος, κόρος to ὕβρις, and ὕβρις to ἄτη or ὄλεθρος. κόρος is *Surfeit*, as in a corn-fed horse who gets 'above himself' and kicks, in ὕβρις, *Insolence* or *Pride*. Aeschylus in his characteristic way develops that into an image—'when a man in Surfeit of Wealth kicks at the great shrine of Right.' ὕβρις was the opposite of Δίκη, Right or Justice, with whom Ἄτη is in alliance ; sometimes Ἄτη is represented as her servant.

'Pride goeth before destruction, and a haughty spirit before a fall': ὕβρις leads to ἄτη—Harm, Destruction, Perdition, Damnation, Ruin, Doom. ὄλεθρος was used in the same sense, and Aeschylus uses βλάβη and πημονή as synonyms of ἄτη: in the two most important passages in Homer about Ἄτη (I 505, T 91) you will find that Ἄτη βλάπτει.

That is the meaning of a phrase in the first chorus (123), the young hares βλαβέντα λοισθίων δρόμων. Hares run in *courses*, δρόμοι: Troy ran nine, she lasted out nine years; but before she could outlast the tenth, the stroke of Ἄτη fell—Ἄτη φθάνει, βλάπτουσα, Homer says—preventing her and disappointing her of her escape.

All these are words in which we must look for a significance when they occur; and there are three others which are significant in this connexion, denoting stages on the road to ruin :—ἐλπίς, Hope, of wrongful gain, Ambition: for example see the chorus in the *Antigone* at line 582, and the passage about Coronis in Pindar, *Pythian* 3. 19. So, to look no further, you will find in more than one place in Thucydides (iii. 45, v. 103) how ἐλπὶς βλάπτει. The other two are θράσος, Hardihood, rash, confident Security; and τόλμα, daring Boldness, Crime, or Sin.

We are in a position now to understand a figurative passage at line 995 of the *Agamemnon* :

> καὶ πρὸ μέν τι χρημάτων
> κτησίων ὄκνος βαλὼν
> σφενδόνας ἀπ' εὐμέτρου—
> οὐκ ἔδυ πρόπας δόμος
> πημονᾶς γέμων ἄγαν.

ὄκνος, hesitation, seems at first sight strange ; we should expect προθυμία, ready willingness ; and what is σφενδόνας ἀπ' εὐμέτρου ?   And surely, it has been argued, πημονᾶς is a mistake for παμονᾶς, possession ? No, it is a synonym of ἄτας, and ὄκνος is merely the contrary of θράσος, and the whole means: '*Now let but timid Caution cast beforehand some of the possession overboard*'—πρὸ μέν τι I suppose must be the reading —'*from the derrick of Proportion*' or '*Due Measure, the whole fabric does not founder through being loaded with surcharge of Harm*'—the Too Much that causes ἄτην.

Well, all that is the moral of the *Persae* ; and the Persian war, as the Greek artists of the time most plainly recognised, was only the Trojan war over again.   We must never forget that this great war between the West and the barbarian East had been the immense event in the life of Aeschylus and his contemporaries, and that both its general moral and its several incidents had been indelibly impressed upon their minds.

The second stanza touches briefly and rapidly upon the stages of the consequence: Peitho, the child of Ate, forces him to commit deadly sin ; when once he has committed it—ὅταν νήκεστον ἀασθῇ in Hesiod's phrase —he is doomed to ruin ; this fond man chasing as it were a winged bird, a proverbial phrase for the pursuit of vain ambitions ; there is our Ἐλπίς, mentioned by allusion ; πτηνὰς διώκεις, ὦ τέκνον, τὰς ἐλπίδας says a fragment of Euripides (271), 'The hopes you chase have wings !'   And he lays the contamination or contagion of his guilt on all his people ; πολλάκι καὶ ξύμπᾶσα πόλις κακοῦ ἀνδρὸς ἀπηύρα Hesiod said (*Op.* 238) in a passage which was learnt in every schoolroom, 'Oftentimes hath a whole state got the evil benefit of one bad man'; as now all Troy has been involved in the guilt of the offender Paris.

Now what is βιᾶται δ' ἁ τάλαινα πειθώ? The critics are not clear; but neither are they much concerned about it; and they pass it over lightly, some suggesting one thing, some another, and not a few with no remark at all. Yet it contains, as I believe, the hidden key to the meaning of Aeschylus in the whole of this great play.

ἄτη is Harm or Ruin, or the blind infatuation—ἄτη βλαψίφρων—that leads a man to commit some rash act which causes ruin. Mythologised, that becomes Ἄτη with an agent, ἀπάτη, Delusion or Deceit, who lays a trap for him, lures him into Ate's toils. This is most definitely stated at the beginning of the *Persae* (*v.* 94):

> δολόμητιν δ' ἀπάταν θεοῦ
> τίς ἀνὴρ θνατὸς ἀλύξει;
> τίς ὁ κραιπνῷ ποδὶ πηδήμ-
> ατος εὐπετέος ἀνάσσων;
> φιλόφρων γὰρ παρασαίνει
> βροτὸν εἰς ἄρκυας Ἄτας,
> τόθεν οὐκ ἔστιν ὑπὲρ
> θνατὸν ἀλύξαντα φυγεῖν,

where φιλόφρων does not, of course, mean with genuine good will, but under the appearance and pretence of it. The whole process is described very accurately according to the Greek conception by Hecate, whose ministers the Witches are, in *Macbeth*: she will

> 'raise such artificial sprites
> As by the strength of their *illusion*   ἀπάτη
> Shall draw him on to his *confusion*:   ἄτη
> He shall spurn fate, scorn death, and bear
> His *hopes* 'bove wisdom, grace, and fear: ἐλπίς
> And, you all know, *Security*   θράσος
> Is mortals' chiefest enemy.'

Πειθώ, Persuasion, Allurement, or Temptation, is another way of expressing the same thing. When Ἄτη is minded to destroy a man, she lays temptation in his path, to induce him to commit some definite and overt act of ὕβρις,—to play, in fact, the part of an *agent provocateur*.

This Πειθώ may be embodied in a human person. There is an excellent illustration[1] in a story told by Herodotus (vi. 135): Miltiades, after Marathon (through ὕβρις) attacked Paros. A priestess there induced him to violate a sanctuary, but by an accident he broke his thigh, was compelled to abandon his project, with its hopes of gold, and shortly afterwards died in disgrace. The Delphian oracle informed the Parians that Timo the priestess was not the true author of these things, but that since it was destined that Miltiades should come to a bad end, she had appeared to guide him on his evil path.

The priestess was the instrument of Ἄτη,—Πειθώ incarnated. To come now to our Aeschylean story, the instrument in Paris' case was Helen. And when I said that in this passage lay, as I believed, the hidden key to the understanding of the play, I meant this further—that the instrument in Agamemnon's case

---

[1] Given to me by Mr F. M. Cornford of Trinity.

is Clytemnestra. Agamemnon falls from precisely the same causes, by precisely the same means, as Trojan Paris; and all the morals of which Paris might appear to be the only subject in their mind the Chorus direct also—more or less consciously—at Agamemnon. That is the large conception which Aeschylus, like the artist that he is, has left to be perceived, one of those lyrical elements running through the play and giving it consistency.

Let us trace that out. Already at the end of the second chorus we have arrived in Agamemnon's case at the same moral as in that of Paris—'Give me the Harmless Mean!' Now let us take the latter part of the third chorus, beginning with the parable of the Lion-cub which symbolises Helen:

ἔθρεψεν δὲ λέοντος ἴ-
νιν δόμοις ἀγάλακτα βού-
τας ἀνὴρ φιλόμαστον,
ἐν βιότου προτελείοις
ἄμερον, εὐφιλόπαιδα
καὶ γεραροῖς ἐπίχαρτον.
πολέα δ᾽ ἔσχ᾽ ἐν ἀγκάλαις
νεοτρόφου τέκνου δίκαν
φαιδρωπὸς ποτὶ χεῖρα σαί-
νων τε γαστρὸς ἀνάγκαις.

χρονισθεὶς δ᾽ ἀπέδειξεν ἦ-
θος τὸ πρὸς τοκέων· χάριν
γὰρ τροφᾶς ἀμείβων
μηλοφόνοισιν ἄταις
δαῖτ᾽ ἀκέλευστος ἔτευξεν·
αἵματι δ᾽ οἶκος ἐφύρθη,
ἄμαχον ἄλγος οἰκέταις,
μέγα σίνος πολυκτόνον·
ἐκ θεοῦ δ᾽ ἱερεύς τις Ἄ-
τας δόμοις προσεθρέφθη.

Here, expressly, Helen is the instrument of Ate ; and the point is enforced by a technical device widely practised in the choral lyric. The stress of the last sentence, which of course would be accentuated in the singing, falls upon the word Ἄτας: now in the previous strophe the word in the corresponding position of emphasis is σαίνων. Attention is thereby called to a

II 1

A young babe Lion, still at breast,
　Was home once by a Herdsman borne,
Housed beneath roof among the rest
　And reared there; in his early morn
And first of age, all gentle, mild,
　Youth's darling, the delight of Eld;
And ofttimes, like a nursling child,
　In arms with happy love was held,
While the weak flesh, demure and bland,
With fawning wooed the fostering hand.

II 2

But age grown ripe, his humour showed
　The born touch that his parents had;
Thank-offering when his nurture owed,
　A banquet, ere the master bade,
With such wild slaughter he prepared,
　It sluiced the dwelling foul with gore,
While helpless, all aghast, they stared
　Upon that bloody mischief sore:—
Divine Will there had found him room,
Housed, to be Priest of slaughtering Doom.

---

correspondence in idea; the Lion-cub or Helen is acting like the ἀπάτη of Ἄτη, which we remember in the *Persae* φιλόφρων παρασαίνει.—For that reason, whatever be the exact reading, and whatever ἔσχε means, I feel sure that φαιδρωπός as well as σαίνων applies to the Lion-cub.—The Chorus continue:

πάραυτα δ' ἐλθεῖν ἐς Ἰλίου πόλιν
λέγοιμ' ἂν φρόνημα μὲν νηνέμου γαλάνας,
ἀκασκαῖον δ' ἄγαλμα πλούτου,
μαλθακὸν ὀμμάτων βέλος,
δηξίθυμον ἔρωτος ἄνθος.
παρακλίνασ' ἐπέκρανεν
δὲ γάμου πικρὰς τελευτάς,
δύσεδρος καὶ δυσόμιλος
συμένα Πριαμίδαισιν,
πομπᾷ Διὸς ξενίου,
νυμφόκλαυτος Ἐρινύς.

παλαίφατος δ' ἐν βροτοῖς γέρων λόγος
τέτυκται, μέγαν τελεσθέντα φωτὸς ὄλβον
τεκνοῦσθαι μηδ' ἄπαιδα θνῄσκειν,
ἐκ δ' ἀγαθᾶς τύχας γένει
βλαστάνειν ἀκόρεστον οἰζύν.
δίχα δ' ἄλλων μονόφρων εἰ-
μί· τὸ δυσσεβὲς γὰρ ἔργον
μετὰ μὲν πλείονα τίκτει
σφετέρᾳ δ' εἰκότα γέννᾳ·
οἴκων γὰρ εὐθυδίκων
καλλίπαις πότμος αἰεί.

III 1

Likewise, arriving once in Ilium town
  What languorous gentleness was seen !
Tranquillest Pearl to shine in Riches' crown,
  With Calm's own soul serene ;
Eyes to send arrowy softness winging fire ;
Loveliness torturing with the heart's desire.

  Then from that Heaven away she fell,
  Transformed into a Fiend of Hell :
  Launched upon Priam's house to bring
  Curse with her sweet companioning ;
  God's Vengeance, in his conduct led
  With ruth about her bridal bed
  And tears for widowed wives to shed !

III 2

There is an ancient proverb men will preach
  As framed by wisdom of old time,
That prosperous Fortune, let him only reach
  To full estate and prime,
Hath issue, dies not childless ; waxen so,
Weal for his heir begets unsated Woe.

  But single in the world I hold
  A doctrine different from the old :
  Not Weal it is, but Sinful Deed
  More sinners after him doth breed
  Formed in his image ; none the less
  Doth lovely offspring always bless
  The house that follows Righteousness.

φιλεῖ δὲ τίκτειν Ὕβρις μὲν παλαιὰ νεά-
ζουσαν ἐν κακοῖς βροτῶν
Ὕβριν τότ᾽ ἢ τόθ᾽, ὅτε τὸ κύριον μόλῃ,
βαθύσκοτον
δαίμονα τίταν, ἄμαχον, ἀπόλεμον,
ἀνίερον θράσος μελαί-
νας μελάθροισιν ἄτας,
εἰδομέναν τοκεῦσιν.

Δίκα δὲ λάμπει μὲν ἐν δυσκάπνοις δώμασιν,
τὸν δ᾽ ἐναίσιμον τίει·
τὰ χρυσόπαστα δ᾽ ἔδεθλα σὺν πίνῳ χερῶν
παλιντρόποις
ὄμμασι λιποῦσ᾽ ὅσια προσέφατο,
δύναμιν οὐ σέβουσα πλού-
του παράσημον αἴνῳ·
πᾶν δ᾽ ἐπὶ τέρμα νωμᾷ.

IV 1

Old Insolence in the evil sort of men
Young Insolence will gender, then or then,
When dawns the appointed hour, a Fiend of gloom
　　For penance, violent, unwithstood,
　　Flushed with such reckless Hardihood
　　　That sin's dark ruinous Doom
　　In black storm on the roof shall rage,—
The latter offspring like his parentage.

IV 2

But Righteousness to the upright heart inclines ;
Bright beneath smoky rafters her light shines :
Gilt-spangled halls, where hands guilt-spotted are,
　　Swift with averted eyes forsakes,
　　Thence to the pure her blessing takes,
　　　To that false lauded star,
　　The Power of Riches, will not bend,
But guideth all things to their proper end.

Enter—Agamemnon; the heir of Tantalus and Pelops, master of the gold-encrusted palace of My-cenae[1], proverbially the wealthiest house among the Greeks, and now enriched with all the added spoil of Troy; to be received with laud and honour and the loud acclamations of the people; ready, like Miltiades and Pausanias after their great victories, for his head to be turned in that same ὕβρις which had ruined the defeated enemy; and now by Justice and Ate to be guided, like Miltiades and Pausanias, to his proper end.

How that is done, and by what agency, we shall see in this same scene—the central scene of the play.

Agamemnon, as I read his opening speech, betrays a spirit of boastful exaltation ill-suppressed. He does indeed acknowledge that the Gods are to be thanked, but he does not say, as it was right for a religious Greek to say, and as our own Henry the Fifth said after Agincourt, 'Give God the praise!' And his expression θεοὺς τοὺς ἐμοὶ μεταιτίους recalls the arrogant inscriptions set up by Pausanias at Delphi and Byzantium[2].

In passing, note the phrase he uses about Troy consuming in the flames:

Ἄτης θύελλαι ζῶσι, συνθνῄσκουσα δὲ
σποδὸς προπέμπει πίονας πλούτου πνοάς.

life vigorous yet
In Doom's fierce hurricane, the expiring ash
Pants forth his opulent breath in puffs of Wealth.

It is the same consequence that Cassandra means

---

[1] Though Aeschylus says merely 'Argos.'
[2] Thucydides i. 132, Athenaeus 536 a.

when later she flings off her golden ornaments and cries :

ἄλλην τιν' ἄτης ἀντ' ἐμοῦ πλουτίζετε.   1267

Endow some other with your fatal Wealth!

1267 ἄτην MS. ἄτης Stanley.

Clytemnestra welcomes him with extravagant laudation, by itself a thing invidious in the sight of men and of the Gods—φθόνος δ' ἀπέστω she exclaims in her ironical hypocrisy ; prostrates herself, or causes her servants to prostrate themselves before him in obeisance —bending to the Power of Wealth—an Oriental form of homage.   No Greek bowed himself before a human king ; the Persians did so ; and this act of προσκύνησις made the Greeks imagine that the Great King was regarded by his subjects as a deity.   And she ends by inviting him to walk upon a path strewn with purple garments, which by the Greeks were kept for the decoration of the Gods.   He well might hesitate ; for to do so would be to assume the divine state of the Persian King, which, as all the audience would remember, was just what only twenty years ago Pausanias had done, and had suffered for it the just retribution. That process is implied in the sinister expression Clytemnestra uses :

εὐθὺς γενέσθω πορφυρόστρωτος πόρος,
ἐς δῶμ' ἄελπτον ὡς ἂν ἡγῆται Δίκη.

Straight let a purple road be laid, and so
Let Justice lead him to his undreamed home!

Agamemnon, who is designed as a well-meaning man, but weak, at first rebukes her for the excessive praise, and then continues :

καὶ τἄλλα μὴ γυναικὸς ἐν τρόποις ἐμὲ
ἅβρυνε, μηδὲ βαρβάρου φωτὸς δίκην
χαμαιπετὲς βόαμα προσχάνῃς ἐμοί,
μηδ᾽ εἵμασι στρώσασ᾽ ἐπίφθονον πόρον
τίθει· θεούς τοι τοῖσδε τιμαλφεῖν χρεών,
ἐν ποικίλοις δὲ θνητὸν ὄντα κάλλεσιν
βαίνειν ἐμοὶ μὲν οὐδαμῶς ἄνευ φόβου.
λέγω κατ᾽ ἄνδρα, μὴ θεόν, σέβειν ἐμέ.
χωρὶς ποδοψήστρων τε καὶ τῶν ποικίλων   917
κληδὼν ἀϋτεῖ· καὶ τὸ μὴ κακῶς φρονεῖν
θεοῦ μέγιστον δῶρον. ὀλβίσαι δὲ χρὴ
βίον τελευτήσαντ᾽ ἐν εὐεστοῖ φίλῃ.
εἶπον τάδ᾽ ὡς πράσσοιμ᾽ ἂν εὐθαρσὴς ἐγώ.   921

Moreover, womanize me thus no more,
Nor fawn me, as I were an Eastern wight,
With grovelling Oes and clamour ; neither strew
Robes on the earth, to call down jealousy.
These are the glorious honours that belong
To Gods ; but human feet on broideries—
'Tis in my conscience fearful. Let your homage
Yield to me not the measure of a God,
But of a man ; the sound on Rumour's tongue
Rings different far of *mats* and *broideries*.
A modest mind's the greatest gift of Heaven.
The name *felicity* 's to keep till men
Have made an end in blessing.—I have said
How I will act herein to feel no dread.

917 This line was explained by Blass *Mélanges Henri Weil* 1898, p. 13.

921 εἰ πάντα δ᾽ ὡς πράσσοιμ᾽ ἂν εὐθαρσὴς ἐγώ. MSS., which could only mean 'if it is the case that (supposing certain conditions) I should act (or 'fare') in all things thus, I have no misgivings.' This can hardly be called a meaning ; nor is ὡς so used in Tragedy. The correction is Weil's : compare *Supp.* 403 εἶπον δὲ καὶ πρίν, οὐκ ἄνευ δήμου τάδε πράξαιμ᾽ ἄν. *Cho.* 684 τοσαῦτ᾽ ἀκούσας εἶπον. *Eum.* 641 τὴν δ᾽ αὖ τοιαύτην εἶπον.

The sentiments themselves are most correct; but they seem to come somewhat mechanically from the mouth, repeated like moral school-texts out of Young's *Night Thoughts.*—Thereupon follows the altercation, the meaning of which has hitherto been so obscure. It requires to be carefully translated; there are several places where we shall go quite astray unless we can translate the Greek correctly:

ΚΛ. καὶ μὴν τόδ' εἰπέ, μὴ παρὰ γνώμην, ἐμοί—   922
ΑΓ. γνώμην μὲν ἴσθι μὴ διαφθεροῦντ' ἐμέ.
ΚΛ. ηὔξω θεοῖς δείσας ἂν ὧδ' ἔρξειν τάδε;   924
ΑΓ. εἴπερ τις εἰδώς γ' εὖ τόδ' ἐξεῖπεν τέλος.   925

Clyt. Tell me now, of your honest mind,—
Agam.   My mind
       Is fixed, and shall not shake.
Clyt.   —in hour of peril
       Would you have made performance of this act
       A promised vow to Heaven?
Agam.   Ay, had advised
       Authority prescribed that holy service.

922 **καὶ μὴν τόδ' εἰπέ** is the preface to a question. **παρὰ γνώμην λέγειν** is 'to say what you do not think'; e.g. Thuc. vi. 9, iii. 42, Plut. *Mor.* 986 B, Dem. 1451. 16: so παρὰ δόξαν or τὰ δοκοῦντα λέγειν, as Plat. *Rep.* 346 A ἐπεὶ τοιόνδε εἰπέ, καὶ μὴ παρὰ δόξαν ἀποκρίνου. *Gorg.* 500 B.—**ἐμοί**, to be emphatic, must have been in the emphatic place, καὶ μὴν ἐμοὶ τόδ' εἰπέ. At the same time, in the personal pronouns at the end we hear an undertone of strife between two wills.

924 **ἔρδειν** MSS. which I correct to **ἔρξειν**: εὔχομαι in the sense '*I vow that I will*' always takes the future. Greek never said ηὔξω ἔρδειν ἂν for 'you vowed that you would,' and ηὔξω ἔρδειν could only mean 'you vowed that you were performing.'—**ἔρδειν** was probably the alteration of a scribe who thought that ἂν and ἔρξειν belonged together.

The editors strangely imagine that ὧδ' ἔρδειν τάδε means 'to refrain from treading on dyed robes'; having forgotten that when you made a vow to the Gods you did not say οὐ θύσω, 'save me, and I will—*not* sacrifice!'

925 **εἴπερ τις εἰδώς γ' εὖ τόδ' ἐξεῖπεν** τέλος Auratus: 'Yes, supposing the

ΚΛ. τί δ' ἂν δοκεῖ σοι Πρίαμος, εἰ τάδ' ἤνυσεν;
ΑΓ. ἐν ποικίλοις ἂν κάρτα μοι βῆναι δοκεῖ.
ΚΛ. μή νυν τὸν ἀνθρώπειον αἰδεσθῇς ψόγον.
ΑΓ. φήμη γε μέντοι δημόθρους μέγα σθένει.
ΚΛ. ὁ δ' ἀφθόνητός γ' οὐκ ἐπίζηλος πέλει.
ΑΓ. οὔτοι γυναικός ἐστιν ἱμείρειν μάχης.
ΚΛ. τοῖς δ' ὀλβίοις γε καὶ τὸ νικᾶσθαι πρέπει.
ΑΓ. ἦ καὶ σὺ νίκην τήνδε δήριος τίεις;   933
ΚΛ. πιθοῦ· κρατεῖς μέντοι παρεὶς ἑκὼν ἐμοί.   934

Clyt.   So; and what think you Priamus had done
            If this achievement had been his?
Agam.   Oh, he
            Had marched upon embroidered tapestry,
            I make no doubt.
Clyt.   For *human* censure then
            Have never a scruple.
Agam.   Yet the tongues of men
            Are potent.
Clyt.   He that moves no jealousy
            Lies beneath envying.
Agam.   'Tis not womanly
            To thirst for contest!
Clyt.   But *felicity*
            Is graced in being conquered.
Agam.   And *thine* eyes,
            Do *they* account such 'conquest' as a prize?
Clyt.   O waive the right, and yield! Of your own will
            Choose to be vanquished, you are victor still.

authority on ritual (the priest, εὖ εἰδὼς μαντευόμενος Hom. β 170) had prescribed
(πιφαύσκων εἶπε or ἐξηγήσατο) this holy service' (τόδε τέλος, which now has a
proper sense).—ἔειπον of the MSS. is the alteration of a scribe who mistook
the construction of εἴπερ τις.—If εἴπερ τις had really meant 'if any one ever did,'
we should have had no γε with εἰδὼς εὖ: yet γε must be genuine, for it was
never inserted by scribes except *metri gratia*: εἴπερ...γε is *siquidem*; in answer
to a question, 'yes; that is, if....'

933 ἦ καὶ σὺ is *tu quoque?* and could not mean anything else.

934 So Weil: Soph. *Aj.* 1353 κρατεῖς τοι τῶν φίλων νικώμενος. The MSS.
give κράτος μέντοι πάρες γ' ἑκὼν ἐμοί.

Vows were made in times of fear or danger (Plato *Laws* 909 E, *Anth. Pal.* IX. 7); you said, *Deliver me from this danger, and I vow to sacrifice* so much; you did not say, *Deliver me, and I vow to refrain from making a costly sacrifice*: the Gods, I fear, would hardly have said, Thank you!

'If occasion had arisen,' says Clytemnestra, 'would you have vowed the Gods this sacrifice?' 'Yes,' replies Agamemnon, 'I would, supposing the authority on ritual'—that is, the priest—'had prescribed it.'—Yes, he would have obeyed unquestioningly, as he had obeyed Calchas when he prescribed the still costlier sacrifice of his daughter's life! The whole scene is *symbolical* of his conduct throughout.—'Very well,' is Clytemnestra's meaning, 'you admit that you would have spent these costly things in sacrifice if there had been occasion: the Gods then can surely see no harm in it; can any human being think it wrong? Would not Priam have done this if he had been in your position?' 'Yes, no doubt,' says Agamemnon, 'Priam would have done it'; and of course what Priam would have done is no example for a Greek; if he consents, he will be acting with just the fatal presumptuousness of Priam. But the woman tempts him, and he yields: πιθοῦ, she says; there we have Ate's Peitho incarnated in Clytemnestra.

She has contrived to make him act like Priam in the impious pride of wealth; forced him to accept the dangerous appellation ὄλβιος, or εὐδαίμων—they were recognised as synonyms—which he had at first repudiated; and at the same time made it clear by using the word ἑκών, that he does so with Free Will.

He attempts to palliate an act which he knows well to be wrong by taking off his shoes, as Orientals did when treading upon holy ground :

ἀλλ' εἰ δοκεῖ σοι ταῦθ', ὑπαί τις ἀρβύλας
λύοι τάχος, πρόδουλον ἔμβασιν ποδός,
καὶ τοῖσδέ μ' ἐμβαίνονθ' ἀλουργέσιν θεῶν
μή τις πρόσωθεν ὄμματος βάλοι φθόνος·
πολλὴ γὰρ αἰδὼς δωματοφθορεῖν ποσὶν   939
φθείροντα πλοῦτον ἀργυρωνήτους θ' ὑφάς.

.   .   .   .

ἐπεὶ δ' ἀκούειν σοῦ κατέστραμμαι τάδε,
εἶμ' ἐς δόμων μέλαθρα πορφύρας πατῶν.

Well, if you must, let presently be loosed
The shoes that do the service of my feet.
            [*A slave unlooses his shoes.*
And as I tread these purple things, I pray
No jealous eye may strike me from afar!
I have much conscience to be prodigal
In squandering Wealth of silver-purchased woofs.

.   .   .   .

So then, being bound and subject to thy pleasure,
Trampling upon purples thus I go.

939 σωματοφθορεῖν MSS. δωματοφθορεῖν Schütz,—a poetical synonym of οἰκοφθορεῖν. This is the scruple that Clytemnestra scoffingly replies to in *v.* 949 sqq.

'Bound and subject to thy pleasure'—Πειθὼ βιᾶται! Forced by Temptation, under foot he treads these beautiful and holy things :—and then, if this had been an opera of Wagner's, with a crash we should have heard the Leit-motiv of Ate.—He proceeds slowly on the purple path towards the palace; and as he goes, Clytemnestra says, still with the same deadly mockery:

ἔστιν θάλασσα, τίς δέ νιν κατασβέσει;
τρέφουσα πολλῆς πορφύρας ἰσάργυρον
κηκῖδα παγκαίνιστον, εἱμάτων βαφάς.
οἶκος δ' ὑπάρχει τῶνδε σὺν θεοῖς, ἄναξ,
ἔχειν· πένεσθαι δ' οὐκ ἐπίσταται δόμος.
πολλῶν πατησμὸν δ' εἱμάτων ἂν ηὐξάμην,
δόμοισι προυνεχθέντος ἐν χρηστηρίοις
ψυχῆς κόμιστρα τῆσδε μηχανωμένῃ.

There is the sea—shall any stanch it up?—
Still breeding, for its worth of silver weight,
Abundant stain, freshly renewable,
For purpling robes withal: nay, Heaven be praised,
The house, my lord, affords us plenty such;
'Tis not acquainted yet with penury.
I had vowed the trampling of a thousand robes,
Had the oracles enjoined it, when I sought
Means for recovery of a life so precious!

Not, of course, 'I had vowed to *refrain* from sacrificing.'—The effect of what she says is 'Surely there is as good purple in the sea as ever came out of it; fresh dye has only to be paid for,—only costs its weight in silver; this great house is surely not going to be ruined for the sake of a few dyed robes!' All that is to impress upon us the nature of his act—the ὕβρις begotten by the Surfeit of great Wealth 'with affluent mansions teeming in excess.'

Later on, Cassandra, whose clairvoyance reads the truth, sees into the heart of Clytemnestra and discerns her plot of the bath and the entangling garment, speaks of her in these terms:

νεῶν τ' ἄπαρχος Ἰλίου τ' ἀναστάτης
οὐκ οἶδεν οἷα γλῶσσα μισητῆς κυνὸς
λέξασα κἀκτείνασα φαιδρόνους, δίκην
ἄτης λαθραίου, τεύξεται κακῇ τύχῃ.

1228

High admiral, proud vanquisher of Troy,
He dreams not, he,
After the fawning speeches long drawn out
By lecherous hound's false tongue, what act it is
With smiling Ate's treachery she designs
For deed in cursed hour!

1228 καὶ κτείνασα MS. κἀκτείνασα Canter: cf. Plat. *Protag.* 329 A ὥσπερ τὰ χαλκία πληγέντα μακρὸν ἠχεῖ καὶ ἀποτείνει 'ring loud and long.'—These lines have suffered grievous treatment at the hands of many critics.

This is a metaphor from what was known as a λαίθαργος κύων, that is, a seeming-harmless dog which turns suddenly and bites, a λαθροδήκτης. Naturally it could be applied to a treacherous person, who in Pindar's words (*Pyth.* 2. 83) σαίνων ἄταν διαπλέκει, while fawning weaves a net of harm, and a line of Sophocles (*fr.* 800) became proverbial in that application, σαίνεις δάκνουσα καὶ κύων λαίθαργος εἶ. He has an allusion to it in another fragment (519), ἡ δ' ἄρ' ἐν σκότῳ λήθουσά με ἔσαιν' ἐρινύς. That, as we have seen already, is the way that Ἄτη acts; and φαιδρόνους is exactly parallel to the φιλόφρων and φαιδρωπός that were used before of Ἄτη and the Lion-cub to describe the fawning blandishments of simulated friendliness.

Clytemnestra speaks herself as follows, in the scene where she confronts the Elders and throws off the mask, frankly avowing her plot and glorying in the details of it:

πολλῶν πάροιθεν καιρίως εἰρημένων 1371
τἀναντί᾽ εἰπεῖν οὐκ ἐπαισχυνθήσομαι·
πῶς γάρ τις ἐχθροῖς ἐχθρὰ πορσύνων, φίλοις
δοκοῦσιν εἶναι, πημονῆς ἀρκύστατ᾽ ἂν
φράξειεν ὕψος κρεῖσσον ἐκπηδήματος;
ἐμοὶ δ᾽ ἀγὼν ὅδ᾽ οὐκ ἀφρόντιστος πάλαι
νείκης παλαιᾶς ἦλθε σὺν χρόνῳ γε μήν·
ἕστηκα δ᾽ ἔνθ᾽ ἔπαισ᾽ ἐπ᾽ ἐξειργασμένοις.
οὕτω δ᾽ ἔπραξα—καὶ τάδ᾽ οὐκ ἀρνήσομαι—
ὡς μήτε φεύγειν μήτ᾽ ἀμύνεσθαι μόρον·
ἄπειρον ἀμφίβληστρον, ὥσπερ ἰχθύων,
περιστιχίζω, πλοῦτον εἵματος κακόν.

All my politic speeches heretofore
Shall nowise make me blush now to confess
The truth and contrary:—how else indeed,
When studying hate's act for one's foe, supposed
One's dear friend,—how else pitch the toils of Harm
To a height beyond o'erleaping?—'Twas not sudden ;
For me, 'twas but
The test and trial of an ancient feud,
Long thought on, and at last, in time, arrived !
I stand here now triumphant, where I struck :—
And so contrived it—I'll avow that too—
As neither should he scape me nor resist :
I wreathed around him, like a fishing-net,
Swathing in a blind maze,—deadly Wealth of robe !

πλοῦτον εἵματος κακόν—that is taken to be merely a fine phrase for abundance of material; surely it implies that the silver-purchased raiment which he trampled in his pride of wealth has now itself, as it were, become the instrument of his undoing, changed into the Net of Ate. This is how Aegisthus speaks when he appears upon the scene to triumph and insult upon his fallen enemy :

ὦ φέγγος εὔφρον ἡμέρας δικηφόρου·   1577
φαίην ἂν ἤδη νῦν βροτῶν τιμαόρους
θεοὺς ἄνωθεν γῆς ἐποπτεύειν ἄγη,
ἰδὼν ὑφαντοῖς ἐν πέπλοις Ἐρινύων
τὸν ἄνδρα τόνδε κείμενον φίλως ἐμοί.

    .   .   .   .

οὕτω καλὸν δὴ καὶ τὸ κατθανεῖν ἐμοί,
ἰδόντα τοῦτον τῆς δίκης ἐν ἕρκεσιν.

O welcome dawning of the day of judgment!
Now will I say the Gods above look down
With eyes of justice on the sins of earth,
When I behold this man, to my dear pleasure,
In woven raiment from the loom of Vengeance

    .   .   .   .

My hour is ripe for death, when here I see
This villain snared within the toils of Justice!

Now, if we turn back again to the *Te Deum*
chanted at the opening of the second chorus, we
may think, perhaps, that we perceive a reason for
the marked insistence on a figure there:

Ὦ Ζεῦ βασιλεῦ, καὶ Νὺξ φιλία,   367
    μεγάλων κόσμων κτεάτειρα·
ἥ τ' ἐπὶ Τροίας πύργοις ἔβαλες
στεγανὸν δίκτυον, ὡς μήτε μέγαν
μήτ' οὖν νεαρῶν τιν' ὑπερτελέσαι
    μέγα δουλείας
γάγγαμον, ἄτης παναλώτου.

O Zeus the King of Heaven! O Night,
With so great splendour and so bright
    Possessed, O friendly Night!
On Troy's renowned high towers was cast
Thy snare, a net so close and fast
    As neither great nor small
Should leap the immense enslaving woof:
Doom's divine drag-net, huge and proof,
    At one sweep took them all!

We have seen, I hope, enough of deep design in Aeschylus to persuade us that he planned this to enforce the parallel with Agamemnon's fate.

So then he lies : πέφανται δ' ἐκτίνουσ' ἀτολμήτων ἀρή :

Under foot when mortals tread
Fair lovely Sanctities, the Gods, one said,
The easy Gods are careless:—'twas profane !
Here are sin's wages manifest and plain,
The sword's work on that swelled presumptuousness,
With affluent mansions teeming in excess,
Beyond Best Measure :—best, and sorrow-free,
The wise well-dowered mind's unharmed Sufficiency !

The Rich man hath no tower,
Whose Pride, in Surfeit's hour,
Kicks against high-enthroned Right
And spurns her from his sight.

Child of designing Ate's deadly womb,
The wretch Temptation drives him to his doom.

WILLIAM RIDGEWAY

THE SUPPLICES OF AESCHYLUS

THE SUPPLICES OF AESCHYLUS.

BAΣ. τί φῂς ἱκνεῖσθαι τῶνδ' ἀγωνίων θεῶν,
λευκοστεφεῖς ἔχουσα νεοδρέπτους κλάδους;
XOP. ὡς μὴ γένωμαι δμωῒς Αἰγύπτου γένει.
BAΣ. πότερα κατ' ἔχθραν ἢ τὸ μὴ θέμις λέγεις;
XOP. τίς δ' ἂν φίλους ὠνοῖτο τοὺς κεκτημένους;
BAΣ. σθένος μὲν οὕτως μεῖζον αὔξεται βροτοῖς.

ll. 304 sqq:

The *Supplices* formed probably the first play in a trilogy, of which the second was either called the *Aegyptii* or the *Thalamopoeoe*, whilst the third was the *Danaides*. The date of its performance is unknown, but there is now a general consensus amongst scholars that it is the earliest of the extant plays of Aeschylus. As the evidence for its date is wholly internal, attempts have been made to fix the chronology of the trilogy from supposed allusions in the *Supplices* to contemporary political events. Thus Boeckh and other older scholars such as Kruse and Ottfried Müller assigned it to the year 461 B.C., that is only three years earlier than the *Oresteia*, on the ground that in that year Athens had formed an alliance with Argos and had a fleet engaged in Egypt. But the Athenian fleet was aiding Egypt against Persia, whereas in the play all is hostility to Egypt, as Prof. Tucker has pointed

out, whilst it is not at all likely that Aeschylus would
have shaped a trilogy simply for the purpose of com-
mending Argos to his countrymen. On the other
hand, Tucker thinks that we may suppose Egypt to
stand for everything that is Oriental, and he accordingly sees in the play an allusion to the threatened
attack of Attica by the Persians, which came to pass
in 490 B.C. He would accordingly place the play in
B.C. 492–1, when the Persian invasion was anticipated,
whilst he thinks that the prayer for Argos—that she
may never be emptied of men—may refer to the disas-
trous defeat suffered by Argos at the hands of the
Spartans in 494 B.C., by which, to use the words of
Herodotus, 'she had been widowed of men.'

But the evidence from style is that on which we
must rely for the early date of the play. Aristotle tells
us in the *Poetics* (IV. 13) that Aeschylus first introduced
a second actor; diminished the importance of the
chorus, and assigned the leading part to the dialogue.
Now as the chief features of the *Supplices* are the great
prominence of the chorus throughout, and the very
subordinate part played by the *rheseis* of the actors,
and the faintness of the character painting of the per-
sonages not members of the chorus, we are led to
believe that the play must have been composed by
Aeschylus not very long after he had made his first
great step, that of adding the second actor and thereby
creating a true dialogue. The prominence given to
the chorus over the actor points to a period when as
yet the drama had advanced but little from the stage
in which Aeschylus took it over from Thespis and
Phrynichus. Thus it is the chorus which parleys

with the king of Argos, although their father Danaus is present at the same time, who might naturally have been expected to speak on their behalf. Moreover, the whole plot centres not on one of the actors, but upon the fate of the chorus of the fifty Danaids. All these considerations show that the play must have been many years earlier than the great trilogy of the *Oresteia*, and must be placed considerably earlier than any of the other extant plays of the poet.

The trilogy deals with the story of the fifty daughters of Danaus who, in order to escape marriage with their cousins the fifty sons of Aegyptus, fled with their aged father to Argos. The *Supplices* deals with their arrival in Argos, their kindly reception in that state, and the repulse of the pursuers. The second play, which was either the *Aegyptii* or the *Thalamopoeoe*, dealt with the return of the sons of Aegyptus in force to Argos, the defeat of the Argives, and capture and forced marriages of the Danaids, and their murder of their husbands, with the sole exception of Lynceus spared by Hypermnestra. The third play contained the trial of Hypermnestra for disobeying her father, and her acquittal when Aphrodite herself came to plead her cause.

As has often been remarked, the *Supplices* cannot properly be termed a tragedy, for there is no catastrophe, and it has a happy ending. Indeed, it contains no thrilling action, nor is there anything in it to rouse the emotions of the modern playgoer except the spectacle of the fifty helpless maidens and their father. Of course it may be urged that there are elements in the play, as in the *Ajax* of Sophocles, which do not appeal to us moderns, but would have acted powerfully upon an Athenian audience. Let us examine the plot of the play and seek to find what these elements may be.

The scene, which remains unchanged throughout the play, lies near the coast south of Argos. In the middle of the stage is seen a mound, probably a tumulus, perhaps once sacred only to the dead that lay within, but later shared by the gods who preside over contests, of whom Zeus, Apollo, Poseidon and Hermes are directly named (193–6). On the mound are wooden images or *xoana* of these gods. At the foot of the mound there is an altar which serves as the *thymele*. The chorus of fifty Danaids in Oriental attire (209), with finely wrought robes, forehead bands and veils, enter bearing in their hands the fresh-plucked olive branches wreathed with wool, that mark them as suppliants (165), and as they advance their leader recites the anapaestic Parodos with which the play opens. The chorus probably consisted not of twelve or fifteen as is often held, but rather (as Tucker has well argued) of the fifty Danaids, for as the chorus speak of themselves as the fifty daughters of Danaus, and as we may suppose that the Athenian audience could count, there would have been a grotesque incongruity between the statement of the chorus and their actual number. Fifty was the original number of the dithyrambic chorus of Arion, and fifty it continued to be according to Pollux down to the time of the *Eumenides*. As the chorus enters their leader recounts how they have fled from Egypt not because they had committed crime, but rather to escape from crime, since they had left the home of their ancestress

Io in order to escape a hated union with their cousins. They pray that Zeus may receive the suppliants, and that the gods may side with them against vice and violence, and they declare that human wantonness is putting forth new leaves. Then Danaus, who has meantime mounted the knoll, cries to his daughters to be prudent, as he sees the dust of a host approaching from Argos, and he urges them to take sanctuary on the mound. The Danaids immediately leave the orchestra and ascend the knoll, invoking the chief gods, whose images they behold.

The king of Argos soon arrives, and demands from what country have they come. He finds it hard to believe that people of their complexion can be Greek, for they are more like Libyans, Egyptians, or Amazons. Then the Danaids convince the king that they are really descended from Io the Argive heroine. He asks why they have sought asylum with the gods of the mound. They tell him that they have fled from marriage with their cousins. Finally the king is moved to send Danaus with suppliant boughs to plead his cause before the people in the city. The king bids the maidens leave their sanctuary, depositing there their boughs, and to descend into the *alsos*. Then the king departs to summon the Argive assembly, and the chorus thereupon pray to Zeus to save them and destroy the Egyptians. Soon Danaus returns alone, having moved the pity of the Argives, for the assembly was of one mind thanks to Zeus working through the eloquence of the king (579–603). Thereupon the chorus pray for the prosperity of Argos. Meanwhile Danaus, who has mounted once more the knoll, is gazing seawards and sees the Egyptians approach. Then he departs to the city to seek aid, and meantime the chorus prays for escape from the loathed embraces of their cousins. Soon enter the Egyptian herald and mariners, and thereupon the Danaids take refuge once more on the mound and cling to the statues. The herald threatens and boasts, and finally he proceeds to lay hands upon them and drag them away by their hair and garments. At this crisis the king of Argos arrives, and after some altercation the Egyptians depart, uttering threats of vengeance on their masters' part, whilst the maidens make their way to the city, where they will find a home.

Let us now examine the reasons given by the chorus for their flight and the grounds on which they claim the pity and protection of Argos. They have left Egypt because they abhor the union with their cousins the sons of Aegyptus (9), they describe the sons of Aegyptus as a lewd swarm (ἑσμὸς ὑβριστής), and pray that they may perish before they mount bridal beds from which immemorial custom debars them:—

> πρίν ποτε λέκτρων ὧν θέμις εἴργει
> σφετεριξάμενον πατραδελφείαν
> τήνδ᾽ ἀεκόντων ἐπιβῆναι.   ll. 37 sqq.

Again the Coryphaeus prays, 'Grant not to youthful lust to find unrighteous consummation, but straightway spurn all wantonness, and bring to happy pass such wedlock as is right' (75), whilst in l. 220 she speaks of the sons of Aegyptus as 'kindred who defile their own race.' Finally she tells the king of Argos that they

have come 'through loathing an unblessed wedlock
there in Egypt' (326). Such then are the moral
grounds urged by the chorus in their plea for
sanctuary.

But surely to an Athenian audience in the time of
Isaeus a more futile plea for succour could not have
been advanced. So far from there being any objection
in that period to the intermarriage of cousins, the law
permitted the marriage of half-brothers and half-sisters
provided they had not the same mother ($\delta\mu o\mu\acute{\eta}\tau\rho\iota o\iota$)
but were sprung from the same father ($\delta\mu o\pi\acute{a}\tau\rho\iota o\iota$).
Moreover at Athens if a man left no son, his daughter
became in a certain sense his heiress ($\dot{\epsilon}\pi\acute{\iota}\kappa\lambda\eta\rho o s$), but
she really, as the term means, was nothing more than
an *adscripta glebae*, an inseparable appendage to the
estate. The next of kin could claim her in marriage,
unless her father had provided otherwise by will. The
heiress was simply the medium for conveying her father's
estate to her own son, for if on her marriage she bore
two sons, the eldest would become the heir to his
father's family, whilst the second might be adopted
into that of his maternal grandfather and on coming
of age, if his grandfather were dead, he would succeed
to the inheritance of which his mother was the heiress.

Not only could the next of kin claim the heiress, if
she was still unmarried, but even if a woman was
already married, and she, by the death of her brother,
became an heiress to the family property, her next of
kin could claim her and could compel her husband
to give her up. Again, if a man after his marriage
became next of kin to an heiress, he might put away
his wife and marry the heiress. Accordingly then

the plea of the Danaids that the marriage with their cousins was incestuous would have excited nothing but contempt in an Attic audience of the time of Demosthenes.

But had this law of the marriage of heiresses always been the custom at Athens or was it but of comparatively recent date? The fact that, even in classical times when succession was through males, the claim of a woman, who had no brothers, to the family land remained paramount points distinctly to a time when all property descended through women.

There were distinct traditions that in old days wedlock was unknown at Athens and that children were named after their mothers. According to Justin[1] it was Cecrops who first established the marriage bond, whilst, according to Varro[2], it was under this same king that the women lost their votes in the assembly, and that the children no longer received the mother's name. Up to that time the women sat in the assembly along with the men. A double wonder sprang out of the earth at the same time, in one place the olive tree, and in another water. The king in terror sent to Delphi to ask what he should do. The god answered that the olive tree signified Athena, and the water Poseidon, and that the citizens must choose after which of the two they would name their town. Cecrops called the assembly; the men voted for Poseidon, the women for Athena, and as there was one woman more, Athena prevailed. Thereupon Poseidon in wrath sent the sea over all the lands of Attica. To

---

[1] II. 6.

[2] *ap.* Augustin. *De civitate Dei* XVIII. 9.

appease the god, the citizens imposed a threefold punishment on their women : they were to lose their votes, the children were no longer to receive the mother's name, and they were no longer to be called Athenians after the goddess. As McLennan points out, this story is a tradition of a genuinely archaic state, and cannot have been the invention of a later time, for Athena in it represents Mother-right.

It is clear now that Athens once had the system of descent through women which prevails still over wide areas of the earth, and which once was the rule in a great part of Europe, for instance, with the ancient Spaniards, and amongst the ancient peoples on the south and east of the Mediterranean, of whom the Lycians are the most typical example. The latter were allied to the Greeks in blood, and with them down to very late times kinship was reckoned through women, the children being called after their mothers, and the property descending through the female line. If a woman cohabited with her slave, the offspring were full citizens, but if a free man lived with a foreign woman or a concubine, even though he was the first in the state, the children had no rights of citizenship, whilst, according to Nicolaus Damascenus, they left their inheritances to their daughters and not to their sons.

It is then certain that at Athens there had once been a time when descent was traced and property passed through females, a fact proved by the circumstance that brothers and sisters by the same father might marry freely, whilst the union of half-brothers and half-sisters sprung from the same mother was considered incestuous. In such a condition of society, marriage outside the kin is the normal rule, that is what is called Exogamy. Plainly then, when the Danaids complain that their cousins are forcing on them an unnatural union, they take their stand on the doctrine of exogamy, whereas at Athens, from the end of the fifth century and after, marriage within the kin is peculiarly favoured, or as McLennan would say, Endogamy was the rule. But as we have just seen that descent through women was once the rule at Athens, there must have been a period of transition from the one system to the other, and there is evidence to show that the older system was still fresh in memory in the time of Aeschylus.

The *Eumenides*[1] furnish us not only with evidence of descent through women, but also show that in the Athens of the fifth century B.C., there was a clear recollection of a time when the marriage tie can hardly be said to have existed at all. When the Furies declare that their office is to drive matricides from their homes, Apollo asks, 'What if he be the slayer of a wife who has murdered her husband?' To this the Furies reply, 'That would not be kindred blood shed by the hands of kindred.' 'Truly,' says Apollo, 'ye make of none effect the solemn pledges of Hera, Teleia, and Zeus. The Cyprian goddess too is flung aside and is dishonoured by this argument, source as she is of the joys dearest to mortals. For the marriage bed, ordained by Fate for husband and wife, is a bond stronger than a mere oath, guarded as it is by Justice.' Again, when Orestes demands of the Furies why they per-

[1] *ll.* 201 *sqq.*

secute him, though they did not pursue his mother, Clytemnestra, in her lifetime for the murder of her husband, they reply that 'She was not of the same blood as the man whom she slew.'

As Athens once had the older system to which the Danaids cling, there must have been a time when the older system gradually gave way to that which we find fully established in the days of the Attic orators. When did this take place ? The question of the transition to succession through males instead of females plays a central part in the *Eumenides*. In that play the dread goddesses, who are maintaining the immemorial customs of the land when indicting Orestes for the slaying of his mother, lay down that the tie between mother and child is especially sacred, whilst Apollo is charged by them with overthrowing primaeval ordinances and introducing strange practices, when, in defence of Orestes, he declares on the authority of Zeus that the tie between the father and the child is much closer. Now, unless the Athenian audience in the year 458 B.C. was fully aware that succession through females had been the ancient practice at Athens, the main point on which the triumphal acquittal of Orestes depends would not have appealed to them in the slightest degree. We are therefore justified in the inference that down to the fifth century B.C. there were many survivals of a time when succession passed through the female line and when the law of exogamy was still a matter of common knowledge to the mass of Athenians.

Now if this was so in 458 B.C. when the *Oresteia* was exhibited, it must have been still more the case when the *Supplices*, supposing that we are right in considering it the earliest extant play of the poet, was composed.   Accordingly the plea of the suppliants to be saved from an endogamous marriage with their cousins would probably appeal to many in the audience who first heard it.   The breaking down of ancient customs cannot be effected in a few years even by a Napoleon, and in an ancient state such as Attica, with its numerous small communities rigidly conservative, the process of change must indeed have been slow and great opposition must have been roused in many quarters by the proposals to alter the time-honoured methods of tracing forms of kinship and succession.

I have already given the plea urged by the chorus against their marriage with their cousins on the ground that such was immoral.   In their conversation with the king of Argos in the lines which it is the object of this paper to expound we find another objection equally strong, one not moral but material.   The king asks them why they have become suppliants of the gods whose images are worshipped at the mound where they have taken sanctuary, bearing their wool-wreathed olive boughs.   The leader replies, ' In order that I may not become the bondswoman of the sons of Aegyptus.'   The king asks, ' Is this merely because there is a family quarrel, or because it is unlawful ? '   She avoids a direct answer by asking 'Who would purchase relations as owners ? '   The king, who is not at all a sentimental statesman, replies, ' It is in this way that men's power becomes aggrandised.'

The Coryphaeus declares that she does not want

to become a bondswoman to her cousins and furthermore she has a great aversion to purchasing with her
property relations who will in reality be her owners.
In this she is simply expressing the feelings of the
Athenian heiresses, who by the new legislation were
to be treated merely as appendages to the family
estate, who could not marry whom they pleased, and
who, even if already married to some other man,
might, under certain circumstances, be torn from their
husbands to gratify the cupidity of the next of kin.

That the poet is alluding to the Attic law relating
to women is rendered all the more probable by the
words of the Argive king (362 sqq.):

εἴ τοι κρατοῦσι παῖδες Αἰγύπτου σέθεν
νόμῳ πόλεως, φάσκοντες ἐγγύτατα γένους
εἶναι, τίς ἂν τοῖσδ᾽ ἀντιωθῆναι θέλοι;
δεῖ τοί σε φεύγειν κατὰ νόμους τοὺς οἴκοθεν,
ὡς οὐκ ἔχουσι κῦρος οὐδὲν ἀμφί σου.

The king says, 'Supposing that the sons of Aegyptus
have authority over you by the law of your city,
alleging that they are your nearest of kin, who would
seek to withstand their right? Needs be that you
must plead according to your own country's laws, that
they have no authority over you.' Now as every
Athenian woman in the later classical period must
have a κύριος, a man who had control over her and
managed her estate, whether father, brother, or next
of kin, the use of the term κῦρος by the king of
Argos is of great significance, and it confirms the view
that the chorus are really voicing the objections made
by the party at Athens, especially women entitled to
property, not only against the innovations by which

they were deprived of managing their estate and marrying whom they pleased outside their kindred, but also against the new proposal by which the heiress was in the power of her next of kin, and thus became in the words of the chorus nothing more than his bondswoman. Now let us turn to the king's reply. To the rhetorical question of the Coryphaeus, 'Who would purchase relations as masters?' the king replies, 'This is the way in which men's power is aggrandised.'

What is the meaning of these words which the Coryphaeus does not attempt to gainsay? They mean nothing more or less than that, as soon as the rule of marriage outside the kin is broken down, the property can be kept within the kin instead of continually passing to the use of men of other families. In this way each *genos* (like the Rothschilds) can increase greatly in wealth and influence. No wonder is it that the Coryphaeus made no reply, for the truth of the king's sententious utterance can be abundantly proved from the history of Mediterranean lands. So long as a tribe is in the hunter state, the rule of exogamy leads to little trouble, for there is no property except some articles of dress, a few weapons and ornaments, and these are usually buried with the dead owners. With the acquisition of domestic animals and the first attempts at cultivation difficulties begin to arise. There is now property to inherit, and that. property passes to the daughters and to the men whom the daughters choose to marry, whilst the sons seek homes for themselves with the daughters of other families, their sisters in some cases at least giving them a dowry in order to help them to obtain eligible *partis*.

This for instance was the usage amongst the ancient Cantabrians in north-west Spain, where we are told by Strabo that the daughters inherited the family property, but that they dowered out their brothers to the women of other families. So long as there is still much un-occupied land no real pinch would be felt by the sons, but when the cultivable land is not of great extent, and it is now practically all under occupation, the position of the sons becomes precarious. A man may or may not secure a wife with a comfortable 'matrimony.' If he does not, he sees the family property pass with his sister or his female cousins to the men of other families, whilst he himself wanders where he may as a lackland. There is only one way in which he can enjoy the family property and that is to marry his cousin or even his sister. Some years ago I pointed out in a public lecture that this was the true explanation of the strange practice of the marriage of brothers and sisters in Egypt, not only in the royal family but also amongst all grades of the population. These marriages were not confined to half-brothers and half-sisters, but as is proved abundantly by documents relating to the payment of taxes whole brothers and whole sisters sprung from the same parents regularly contracted marriages. When therefore the Ptolemies married their sisters, it was not through a mere freak of depravity, but was completely in conformity with the usage of their subjects.

It is now clear that in the transition from succession through females to that through males, which we find in the time of Isaeus and Demosthenes, there must have been a breaking down of the principle of exogamy. It is not unreasonable to suppose that the first attacks on an immemorial social institution of such primary importance would arouse the strongest feeling and would only finally succeed after long struggles.

A consideration of the law of inheritance in two other countries of the Eastern Mediterranean will show us probably the steps which led up to the position of women, such as we find it to be at the end of the fifth century at Athens. In Lycia we saw that if a free woman had a child by her slave, it was perfectly legitimate, and if a daughter, it would inherit the family property. At Athens the heiress was nothing more than an appendage inseparably attached to the family inheritance. The famous Gortyn laws may show us some of the steps by which probably Attic law relating to heiresses advanced to the stage at which we find it in the days of the Orators. Thus at Gortyn, although the sons had the sole right to the town house, its furniture, and the cattle, the daughters shared in the rest of the inheritance, each daughter getting half as much as a son. If a girl was an heiress ($\pi\alpha\tau\rho\omega\iota\hat{\omega}\kappa\circ\varsigma$), she might marry whom she pleased within the limits of her tribe, if she was content with the town house, and half the remainder of the estate, the next of kin taking the other half. If there was no next of kin, the heiress might marry any one of her tribe who would have her; if not, the law lays down that she may marry whom she can. Again, if a married woman became an heiress, she was not compelled to leave her husband, although she could do so if she pleased. If she divorced her husband she was not always free to marry whom she pleased : for if she was childless she must either marry the next of kin, or indemnify him ; but if she had already children, she might marry any member of her tribe who would have her. So too with a widow, if she became an heiress. Though at Athens it was obligatory on the next of kin either to marry the heiress, or to provide her with a dower if she were poor, there was no such obligation at Gortyn, for the next of kin was not compelled to marry the heiress if he gave up his claim to the estate. Again, whereas at Athens the property of the heiress became the property of her son as soon as he came of age, at Gortyn the mother had the same rights over her property that her husband had over his, and as long as she lived her children could not divide her property against her wish. At her decease it was transmitted in the same way as the estate of a man. Finally at Gortyn an heiress under certain circumstances could marry a serf and the offspring would be legitimate.

As the Lycians were closely connected in blood with Crete, and in fact are said to have been emigrants from that island, it would seem that in the Gortyn laws respecting the property of heiresses which show far more consideration for the rights of women than those of Athens we have not an outcome of more enlightened legislation, as is held by Mr Jevons, but rather the result of an attempt to advance in the same direction as that made by the men at Athens, though in Crete the men either did not desire or had not been able to encroach so much on the ancient rights of the women. The Gortyn code shows us really an earlier stage in the transition from exogamy to endogamy than that

seen at Athens, and we may not be wrong in holding
that the first steps taken at Athens may not have been
unlike what we find as the actual state of things in
Crete or at least at Gortyn.

Let us return to the lines under discussion. The
meaning of the answer of the king of Argos to the
Danaids is now clear. 'You may not,' says he, 'like
being compelled to marry your kinsmen, but all the
same it is best for the kin, for the family property will
thereby be kept together, and consequently its power
and influence will increase.'

When once we realise that the change over from
female to male kinship was a burning question at
Athens in the first half of the fifth century, being
still of sufficient interest to form the central feature in
the third play of the great trilogy of the *Oresteia* in
458 B.C., we can readily understand that the audience
which listened to the *Supplices* in the opening decades
of that century found in its plot a theme of absorbing
interest for them, but which would have aroused just
as little feeling in the days of Demosthenes as it does
in ours.

Now what was the attitude of Aeschylus himself
towards these social innovations? It has always been
the fashion amongst scholars to speak of the poet as a
great religious and political conservative, but I venture
to think a re-consideration of the question will lead us
to a different conclusion. Briefly stated the grounds for
the ordinary belief are (1) his oft-repeated reverence for
Zeus and the other gods, and (2) his eulogy on the
Areopagus. Yet investigation will show us that the
great dramatist so far from being a conservative was

the great proclaimer of a new religious and social gospel. It is perfectly true that from first to last the power of Zeus and the gods is constantly reiterated in all his plays. Thus in the *Supplices* itself, probably his earliest extant work, the chorus at the very outset invokes the aid of Zeus, and elsewhere in the play Zeus is described as the helper of the helpless, as he that helps to right them that suffer wrong, as the all-seeing one, whose eyes behold all that is done upon earth, and finally as the judge of the wicked after death. Zeus, Apollo, Poseidon and Hermes, in the order given, have statues on the sacred knoll, where the chorus took sanctuary. From the standpoint of Aristophanes and his contemporaries Aeschylus may indeed be regarded as a conservative. But is he so when judged in relation to his own time ? Were Zeus and Apollo gods of immemorial reign at Athens? The poet himself tells us explicitly in the *Prometheus Vinctus* that new gods have arisen which have upset the ancient order of things, and these new gods especially are Zeus, the overthrower of the Titan brood, and his son Apollo. In the *Eumenides* the Erinyes complain that Zeus and Apollo are upsetting the old order of things, whilst they declare that they themselves are trying to uphold the ancient customs of the land, such as kinship traced through the mother. The dramatist could never have dared to speak thus of Zeus and Apollo unless his audience were well aware that the two great deities were but new-comers into Athens. Moreover a striking confirmation of the statement of Aeschylus is furnished by an examination of the shrines of the gods at Athens. Though, as we know from Homer, Athena had her home on the Acropolis in the 'strong house of Erechtheus,' yet down to the latest days neither Zeus nor Apollo had a temple on that famous citadel. Though Zeus in later times had managed to annex an altar in front of the north door of the Erechtheum, down to the last he never could find entrance into the great temple itself, in which Athena and Poseidon reigned. Again the names of the temples built in honour of Zeus and Apollo in other parts of the city show clearly that they were adventitious and not indigenous deities. That of Zeus was called the Olympieum, whilst those of Apollo were termed respectively the Pythium and the Delphinium, showing that the cult of Zeus was derived from Olympus in Thessaly, whilst that of Apollo had been introduced from Delphi.

Moreover, the Zeus temple was not of ancient date, for we know that it was begun by the despot Peisistratus in the plain south-east of the Acropolis about the middle of the sixth century B.C., but so indifferent as a whole were the Athenians to the worship of the Olympian, that whilst Pericles lavished vast sums on the Parthenon, and even when utterly exhausted towards the close of the Peloponnesian War the Athenians spent a large sum in rebuilding the Erechtheum—the home of Athena and Poseidon—yet the temple of the Father of gods and men, though almost completed by the munificence of Antiochus Epiphanes 174 B.C., was not finished until the reign of Hadrian.

So far then from Aeschylus being a conservative in religion, he is the champion of the gods Zeus and Apollo against the dread dark beings revered in primitive Athens, which are upheld by the Eumenides in the play named after them. The Furies held that there could be no mercy for the shedding of kindred blood, but Apollo on the authority of his father Zeus proclaims that the sinner after due purification can meet with pardon and forgiveness. Again, in that same play, though Athena is made to declare herself altogether the child of Zeus, yet at no distant date, as we know from Herodotus, she had been always held to be the daughter of Poseidon, who continued down to the last, as we have just seen, to share with her the Erechtheum. According to Herodotus it was only quite late that she became wroth with Poseidon, repudiated him as her father and affiliated herself to Zeus. Nor are we without some hint as to the time and cause for the introduction of the new doctrines into Athens. We have just seen that it was Peisistratus who laid the foundations of the temple of Zeus, and it is familiar to all scholars that it was under that same despot that the study of the Homeric poems assumed an active form at Athens. In these poems, though Athena may play a prominent part, Poseidon is but of very secondary rank, whilst Zeus the All-father and Apollo his son are the chief divinities of the Acheans. In these poems likewise descent was reckoned by males amongst the Acheans, and the sanctity of the marriage tie holds a foremost place as, for instance, in the case of Penelope. So far then from Aeschylus being a conservative in religion, he was the proclaimer of a new gospel which centred round Zeus and Apollo whose Testament was the *Iliad* and the *Odyssey*.

To Aeschylus the religious conceptions of the Homeric poems and their loftier morality came as a revelation. In the old world of which the Eumenides were the champions the worship of the dead, that is of the mere local ancestor, was all-pervading. To the imagination of Aeschylus the Achean Zeus, the over-thrower of the Titans and all the dark powers which had brooded over primaeval Athens, was a perfect illumination. Instead of narrow local fetish cults of dead heroes and heroines came the conception of the All-father, the All-seeing one, whose eyes were in every place beholding both the evil and the good, and helping them to right that suffer wrong, punishing the guilty, yet having mercy and forgiveness for them that deserved it. Henceforward with him, although the spirits of the dead that dwell in the graves beneath the earth may be capable of wreaking dreadful ven-geance, yet there was a greater power whose force and controlling influence was as wide as the firmament itself.

Yet the Achean gods had not merely brought into Athens a gospel of mercy and forgiveness for the sinner, but along with their cult came a social doctrine strange and repulsive to the ancient goddesses of the land. When Apollo asks the Eumenides why they had not punished Clytemnestra for murdering her husband, they reply that as he was of a different *genos* from hers, it was not a case of the shedding of kindred blood. Apollo answers, 'What, are the sacred pledges of Hera, Teleia and Zeus of none effect in your eyes, nor those of Aphrodite, the giver of the greatest joys to men?'

In other words Apollo is simply urging the

doctrine of the sanctity of marriage as seen amongst the Acheans of Homer. On the other hand in Hesiod the marriage bond is unknown amongst the gods, but as Aristotle says that men make not merely the forms of the gods like unto their own, but also their lives, we may infer that, with the people amongst whom the *Theogony* was shaped, the marriage bond was but of a lax form. But as amongst the Homeric Acheans the marriage bond is held sacred, we may have little doubt that the ἱερὸς γάμος, the sacred rite of marriage, celebrated between Zeus and Hera, each year at Argos, and probably in every community in Greece, was the outcome of the religion of Zeus. It is clear from the discussion between the Eumenides and Apollo that the marriage bond was not held sacred in ancient Athens, but that it was only introduced along with the worship of Zeus and Apollo. But as succession through males is only possible when the marriage bond has been firmly established, the final decision of Athena in the *Eumenides* in favour of closer affinity of the child to the father than to the mother is but a natural corollary to the doctrine of the sanctity of marriage.

Let us now return to the trilogy of which the *Supplices* is held to be the first play. We saw that although the conclusion of that drama pointed to the triumph of the ancient doctrine of marriage outside the kin, yet in the second play the tables were turned, for the sons of Aegyptus vanquished the Argives and captured the daughters of Danaus. It probably also contained the forced marriage of the maidens with their cousins and the murder of all the husbands save Lynceus spared by the *splendide mendax* Hypermnestra. Then came the third play, the *Danaides*, in which the trial of Hypermnestra for disobeying her father and sparing her young consort was probably the central feature. We know for certain that Aphrodite herself came forward as advocate for Hypermnestra and triumphantly vindicated her action, on the ground that she was completely justified by love towards her young husband.

We have just seen that Apollo in the *Eumenides* asks the Erinnys had she no regard for the sacred marriage rites of Hera and Zeus and for Aphrodite. Here in the earlier trilogy Aeschylus himself had already justified the breaking down of an artificial social system by the all-conquering power of love. Aeschylus was then no rigid conservative, but rather the apostle of a new and loftier religion, the proclaimer of a nobler and a purer morality, and the advocate of a more advanced and stable social system.

www.ingramcontent.com/pod-product-compliance
Ingram Content Group UK Ltd.
Pitfield, Milton Keynes, MK11 3LW, UK
UKHW042152280225
455719UK00001B/299